ASSESSING ATHLETIC AND PHYSICAL EDUCATION PROGRAMS

Assessing Athletic and Physical Education Progams:

A Manual with Reproducible Forms

KENNETH A. PENMAN, Ph. D.
SAMUEL H. ADAMS, Ed. D.

Department of Physical Education
Washington State University

Allyn and Bacon, Inc.
BOSTON   LONDON   SYDNEY

Contents

Preface and Acknowledgments

This assessment manual for athletic and physical education programs and personnel is primarily a manual of assessment instruments. These assessment instruments have been designed to develop a profile of a program or specific personnel within a program. The profile of a program or personnel should identify both strengths and weaknesses. It is the intent of the authors that these profiles should be used as diagnostic tools to give guidance for the strengthening of programs and personnel, not as a tool for firing personnel or deemphasizing programs. Strengths should be acknowledged, and the weaknesses revealed should be used as a base to formulate future planning to strengthen these portions of the profile. The instruments may be used by a team of evaluators or for self-evaluation. Another purpose of these instruments, because of the comprehensiveness of the instruments themselves, is to reveal many aspects of the program not commonly known and of responsibilities of personnel not usually considered whenever they are evaluated. This program should provide a much broader concept and base for evaluation—much broader than the common win-loss concept of success.

The manual is divided into five parts. Part One deals with the introduction to assessment in athletics and physical education and how to use the assessment instruments in the manual. It also includes the analysis of the results of assessment. This part should be read first and very carefully, particularly by the person in charge of the evaluation program, as it is pertinent to the assessment instruments in the rest of the manual. In addition, information and suggestions on who should use the various assessment instruments is included.

Part Two consists of the assessment instruments for athletic personnel. Part Three includes assessment instruments of the athletic program.

Assessment instruments for physical education programs and personnel are found in Part Four.

Part Five (appendix) includes sample job descriptions and announcements.

The manual has been designed to be used on any educational level (junior high school, high school, junior college, college, or university) with any sport (either sex) and personnel of either sex. The questions that do not apply to a specific level or situation are simply to be ignored. Most questions demand a response on a rating contiuum of 1 to 7, with 1 being the lowest and 7 the highest. Some questions can simply be answered "no" or "yes."

Educational administrators especially will find the manual valuable. However, all personnel involved in the programs will probably find it valuable for self-evaluation, as well as looking at the programs they are responsible for with a more comprehensive view. The manual could also be used as a textbook or supplemental textbook in certain classes such as Administration of Physical Education and Athletics, evaluation courses, curriculum, etc.

The manual does not take a philosophic direction. It might be helpful, therefore, for each evaluator to have a written statement of the program's or the person's philosophy and/or objectives being evaluated.

The authors wish to express their appreciation to Dick Watters, Bill Bleakney, Pedro Gomez, Phil Hirsch, Becky Baker, Don Anderson, Amanda Burk, Steve Epperson, Donna Kasari, Kathleen Mattson, Linda Murphy, Dan Rusch, and Al Sanders, who contributed to this work. The contributions of Tom Mays and John Reeg in validating certain of the instruments were very valuable. The authors also deeply appreciate the time and effort of Jeanette Johnson and Kathy Timson, typists of the manuscript.

PART ONE

Assessment Needs and Objectives

CHAPTER 1

Introduction to Assessment
in Athletics and Physical Education

In the past decade the education profession has experienced a renewed emphasis on evaluation of performance and procedures used to teach children. This renewed emphasis on evaluation has increased the need for better evaluation instruments, competent test administrators, and qualified evaluators of test results. Every area in education is being affected. Since education is supported by the public tax dollar, the community has become more familiar and involved in education and is demanding more accountability. The term *accountability* has recently been associated with the system that mandates that educators must state their objectives, suggest an efficiency level, and demonstrate that a majority of the students have achieved the suggested efficiency level. One of the positive aspects of this system is that it makes the public cognizant of the objectives of a program and, therefore, gives them a broader and more realistic basis and understanding for evaluation of the program.

One of the educational programs the public has intuitively evaluated for years is the athletic program. Because of the lack of stated objectives for athletics or the fact that in most cases the stated objectives have not been made known to the public, the primary indicator for the success of sports programs in schools has been win-loss records. In the same manner coaches have been evaluated by the public more than most educators because their "success" is based on a win-loss record and this success-failure evaluation is exposed to the public weekly. If a coach is a consistent "loser" according to a win-loss record, he/she usually does not keep his/her job very long.

In recent years more formal education techniques have been developed for the evaluation of athletics. These evaluation techniques delve much deeper into their assessment analysis than merely looking at win-loss percentages. The intent of this manual is to incorporate the latest developments in assessment for analyzing all phases of athletic and physical education programs, including personnel, into a usable reference for school officials, athletic directors, coaches and teachers.

WHO EVALUATES?

Everyone believes himself/herself to be an expert in evaluating athletics! Since athletics are in front of the public constantly and because they trigger strong emotional responses from spectators, everyone assumes a role in evaluating the coach, the athletic program, and/or a specific athletic sport. In fact this informal type of evaluation seems to be a favorite American pastime. However, it is also well known that there is not always close agreement among individuals on their evaluations. This type of assessment depends on the viewpoint of the person doing the evaluation. The evaluator may be the parent of an athlete, an athlete, the local sports news reporter, the coach, other coaches, the principal, the athletic director, the superintendent, the alumni association, the school board, the "superfan," or perhaps a combination of these, such as a parent who is also a school board member.

THE EDUCATIONAL PERSPECTIVE ON ASSESSMENT

When appraising athletics in schools, our analysis must come from the viewpoint that athletics is a part of the educational system of the society. To do otherwise would lead us to include, in addition, an analysis of amateur and professional sports, which is far beyond the intended scope of this manual. The basic assumption underlying this manual is that athletics in schools is an integral part of the educational process and, therefore, should be evaluated as such.

Education has been defined in many ways. In this manual we shall use the following simplified statement as our working definition: Education is the process whereby intentional direction is given to the full, wholesome development of human beings. From this concept of education, specific goals can then be established to fulfill this objective. Physical Education is merely one way of meeting the goals of education by using a variety of motor activities, integrated with cognitive skills, to change behavior. Often games or contests are used for this purpose. In order to develop youth to their fullest, opportunities must be provided that allow the exceptionally well-skilled individuals to develop their potential. Athletic programs in schools provide such an opportunity.

EDUCATION IS A DYNAMIC PROCESS

Fortunately, the educational process is continually changing—hopefully for the betterment of society—as new information, new methods, and new processes are developed. Essentially, this cycle involves: (1) establishing goals by society (the nation and the community), (2) identifying specific programs to meet the stated goals, (3) implementing specified programs, (4) assessing established programs (the purpose of this manual), and (5) reviewing goals and reestablishing the goals if change is imminent.

Applying this process to athletics, we may have something like:

1. The community says, "we want a winning sports program."
2. Staff, facilities, and equipment are procured by the school board to establish the specific sports programs.

3. Students are encouraged to become part of the program, and the program is implemented.
4. The sports program is evaluated (unfortunately, this often consists of only a win-loss percentage).
5. Goals are reevaluated and either changed or reinforced.

WHAT ARE YOUR GOALS?

There is an old axiom that says, "If you don't know where you are going, any road will get you there." We might rephrase this saying, "If you don't have any stated goals for your physical education and athletic program, any kind of program will do." If there are no stated goals, assessment lacks clarity and direction because anything that exists is satisfactory. It doesn't even matter whether you win or not, since "winning" has not been stated as a goal! If the goal *is* only to win, then any means necessary to accomplish winning is permissible and the only assessment necessary is to examine the win-loss percentage.

Therefore, it is essential to have a statement of goals for the physical education program in general and for each specific portion of the program before any assessment can be made as to "how good" the total program is. Where personnel are concerned, specific job descriptions *must* be established for each position, so that the teacher-coach knows what is expected of him/her; in addition, his/her performance can be evaluated, based upon the written job descriptions. (Sample job announcements and job descriptions are included in the appendix.)

SAMPLE GOAL STATEMENTS

A. Athletic program goals established by a State Federation:
  1. To provide athletic activities based on the needs of potential participants.
  2. To develop good citizenship and respect for rules and authority.
  3. To provide opportunities to develop physical excellence.
  4. To develop an understanding of the value of cooperation and competition.

B. Athletic program goal statement established by a school district:
  1. The interscholastic athletic program provides an opportunity for maximum development of the gifted performer. Therefore, the interscholastic athletic program is not intended for participation by all students, but rather for those who are physically and emotionally capable of highly skilled competition. The objective of the athletic program is to win within the spirit of the rules.

C. Goals established for a baseball program:
  1. To develop "high level" student athletes.
  2. To represent, with pride, the students of the school, the athletic department, community, families, and team.
  3. To develop the individual socially, intellectually, emotionally, and athletically.
  4. To develop team consciousness.
  5. To develop skills that will allow the individual to compete at a high level.
  6. To learn how to be a winner.

D. A head football coach job description:
1. He should have the ability to plan and implement a total high school football program.
2. He should have the ability to select and work with assistants in an efficient manner.
3. He shall possess the ability to implement a practice schedule that will result in maximum productivity.
4. He shall possess the ability to plan and implement a strategy for success in contests.
5. He shall possess leadership abilities, a desire to win, a compassion for individual differences, and an understanding of the value of each student as a human being.

These examples are simply excerpts from more descriptive lists of objectives that, in essence, describe the goals of the total athletic program in schools. They should, of course, be more complete and detailed. However, regardless of how "good" the goals are or how much you agree with the philosophy, the *program, as stated,* can be evaluated. Referring to Goal A-1, we can determine if the athletic program is, in fact, meeting the students' needs. In B we can evaluate whether students are being taught to "win within the spirit of the rules." In C-2 we can evaluate the conduct of baseball players at school, in the community, and on trips. In D-3 we can evaluate whether the coach has been effectively implementing practice sessions for maximum productivity.

Although we may, under the framework of education, philosophically debate the value of any stated goal for the program, those taxpayers who support the schools will ultimately determine, through elected school board members, the actual goals for the sports program. We can, however, examine objectively the component parts of the program and personnel and thereby assess their worth within the framework of stated goals.

THE ATHLETIC ASSESSMENT MODEL

Physical education is usually included in a total school curriculum evaluation model. Less frequently, however, is assessment of athletics (a part of physical education) included in these models.

The following diagram provides a model for assessing the athletic program of a school district. The initial impetus arises from a desire to assess. *This is a big hurdle!* Many people are threatened by merely learning that they are going to be evaluated or that "their" sports program is going to be evaluated. Others welcome the opportunity to see how well they are doing so that they can improve their performance and/or program. The desire to assess the program is initiated by information received from noting educational trends relating to self-assessment, forced evaluation by some accreditation agency, or by public opinion in the form of intuitive feedback. Once the decision is made to assess the program, all existing goal statements must be ferreted out. The program areas to be evaluated need to be identified as well as the personnel involved in all aspects of the program. A synthesis is then made of the assessment, and recommendations made for changing goals to meet practices or changing practices (and possibly personnel) to meet goals.

The evaluation instruments developed in this manual are not primarily intended for use as justification for "getting rid of someone." They are designed to be used to assess programs and personnel in their formative stages rather than for terminal evaluation.

Chapter 2 will describe the basic method of using the evaluation instruments. Chapter 3 will explore how to utilize the results of the assessments in a meaningful and useful way.

ATHLETIC ASSESSMENT MODEL

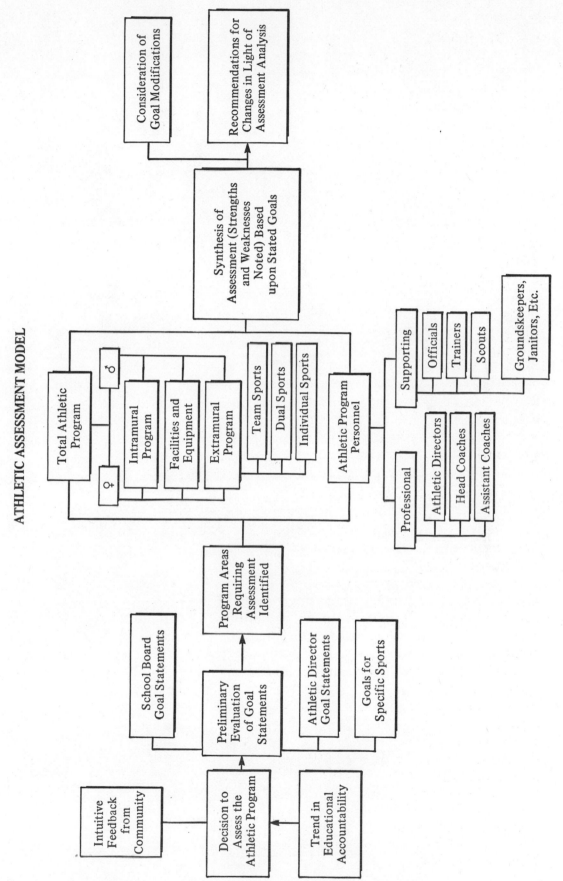

How to Use the Assessment Forms

INTRODUCTION

The purpose of assessing programs and personnel in athletics and physical education should be viewed as a formative process, that is, a process that has as its primary intent—improvement. Methods of using the information will be described in Chapter 3. It is appropriate to explain some of the background of the development of the assessment instruments. In addition, suggestions will be given about how to use the assessment system.

In the process of developing assessment instruments, it became apparent that it would be necessary to develop either a few general instruments or to develop a large number of specific instruments. For example, Part Two contains an evaluation instrument for the head coach. An alternative would have been to develop a separate instrument for the head football coach—men; the head swimming coach—women; and so on. The former was chosen as the format for this assessment system. General traits that are deemed important for anyone (male or female) who is responsible for heading a sports team are included in this one evaluation instrument.

In addition to the fact that a variety of sports are subject to being assessed in both men's and women's programs, there exist differing needs for different levels of education. Should, for example, the head football coach be evaluated in a similar manner if he is in the middle school, high school, community college, small college, or university?

In order to eliminate the need for hundreds of different evaluation instruments, an attempt was made to make each evaluation instrument general, but extensive. All the factors that seemed important in an assessment instrument for each kind of sport and for each type of staff member are included. As a result, there will be a few (and sometimes many) statements to consider that *do not apply* to your situation. The answer to this is simple—*don't use them!* When the evaluation instrument is typed for duplication purposes, simply omit the items that are not applicable to your level or situation.

Most statements have been formulated so that little research is needed for the evalua-

tors to make their assessment. Therefore, some of the evaluation may consist of *opinion**
Occasionally, where *facts* are necessary but unobtainable, the evaluator can omit that
phase of the evaluation. In addition, if the evaluator has insufficient knowledge to give an
opinion, he/she should not respond to that portion of the instrument.

WHO SHOULD EVALUATE?

In the previous chapter a few people who should evaluate were identified. With more
formal evaluation procedures, those evaluating the program need to be carefully selected.
An assessment could be done by a single evaluator. A better procedure, of course, would
be to have a variety of evaluators give input. When a corporate evaluation is made, individual
biases (positive or negative) are deemphasized and a more well-rounded and valid appraisal
can be made. *The nature of the evaluating group and the number of each kind of member
also needs to be carefully considered.* For example, you may not wish to have the same
people evaluate both the athletic director and the women's swimming program. The following is a list of people who should be considered when determining the individuals to be
used to evaluate a sports program, part of a sports program, or personnel involved in the
sports program.

president	students
superintendent	athletes
principal	board members
dean	community support members
department chairperson	parents
athletic director	activity director
head coaches	alumni
assistant coaches	person being evaluated

Consideration should also be given to the number of people used from each of these
categories. For example, how many students, athletes, and/or parents should be considered?
How many other coaches should be considered, and so on? Since random sampling techniques cannot be applied here, special care needs to be given in an attempt to eliminate
bias in selecting evaluators. In order to get a fair assessment, all viewpoints should be considered. Intentionally "loading" the evaluation group with people known to be highly in
favor of a person or program, or against a person or program, makes the assessment procedure a great waste of time and constitutes questionable ethical behavior. In addition, consideration should be given to the weight assigned to each evaluator. Will the student and
athletic director have an equal chance to rate? Table 1 suggests people that may be appropriate to evaluate each specific instrument.

SELF-EVALUATION

Probably one of the most meaningful uses of the evaluation instruments for personnel
is that of self-analysis. By going through each specific statement, people can evaluate how

---

*When factual data are readily available, they should by all means, be utilized.

Table 1

Suggested Personnel for Evaluating Each Instrument

Person or Program Being Evaluated	President	Superintendent	Principal	Dean	Department Chairperson	Athletic Director	Head Coach	Assistant Coach	Student	Athlete	Board Members	Community Support Member	Parent	Activity Director	Alumni	Teacher
Athletic Director		X	X	X	X	X	X	X	X	X	X	X	X	X	X	X
Head Coach		X	X	X	X	X	X	X	X	X	X	X	X	X	X	X
Assistant Coach			X	X	X	X	X	X	X	X	X	X	X		?	?
Official			X			X	X	X								
Athletic Trainer						X	X	X	X	X	X		X		X	
Athletic Program	X	X	X	X	X	X	X	X	X	X	X	X	X	X	X	X
Specific Sport Programs			X		X	X	X	X	X	X		X	X		X	X
Facilities	X	X	X	X	X	X	X	X	X	X	X	X	X	X	X	
Legal Aspects		X	X	X	X	X	X									
Physical Education Instructor			X	X	X				X				?			
Physical Education Program			X	X	X	X	X	X	X			X	X	X	X	X
Intramural Program			X	X	X				X			X	X	X	X	X
Physical Education Chairperson			X	X	X	X	X	X	X					X		X

11

Copyright © 1980 by Allyn and Bacon, Inc. Reproduction of this material is restricted to use with *Assessing Athletic and Physical Education Programs: A Manual with Reproducible Forms* by Kenneth A. Penman and Samuel H. Adams.

effective they are and thus see where improvement is needed. They may also possibly become aware of practices and/or procedures they are using that have become obsolete or illegal.

CONFIDENTIALITY OF RESULTS

In order to receive valid opinions on the evaluations, it is essential to insure evaluators that their opinions will be kept confidential. If names are not placed on the evaluation instrument, standard return envelopes are enclosed, and a "neutral" collecting agent is utilized, confidentiality is assured to a greater degree, and evaluators are more likely to give honest and frank opinions. Consideration must also be given, at the initiation of the assessment program, to a policy stating who will see the results.

RATINGS

For all instruments relating to programs or personnel, a standard response rating of 1 to 7 is used. The seven represents a very high opinion, a rating of one represents a very poor opinion, and a rating of four should be considered an average response for that trait. No response means that the evaluator did not feel competent to give an opinion on that specific trait or he did not have the information necessary to make a response. Do not feel that all rating aspects or questions included in the instrument need to be completed. Many may not apply to your situation.

Each evaluation form will have a major category utilizing a Roman numeral. Under that major category will be subcategories utilizing the capital letters. Following the subcategories there will be a space for rating on the 1 to 7 point scale. Under each of those subcategories there are numerous statements for consideration in making a final rating for the subcategory. These statements are numbered, using Arabic numerals. Following these statements, ratings on the 1 to 7 point scale are provided (only for convenience in estimating the subcategory rating). Occasionally an alternate response may be required. If the response is *no*, the evaluator should circle the 1. If the response is *yes*, they should circle the 7. If each statement that the evaluator is qualified to evaluate is checked, it will assist the evaluators in making a final, more objective assessment of that subcategory. On the final assessment profile (explained in the next chapter), the major category rating will be determined by your plotting each subcategory rating on the profile.

Directions are included at the beginning of each assessment instrument. When the evaluation coordinator receives the completed ratings, the subcategories are averaged and plotted on the profile.

WHAT TO EVALUATE

This manual includes instruments for assessing athletics including: the total athletic program; a specific (team, dual, or individual) sport; personnel, including the athletic director, head coach, assistant coach; officials; and athletic trainers. In addition, an evaluation

Figure 1

Assessment of the Head Coach (example)

III.   The Coach As a Person

A. Personal Qualities   1 2 3 ④ 5 6 7
Comments
    The coach:
    1. has high moral values.   1 2 3 ④ 5 6 7
    2. sets a positive example in work, deed, and appear-   1 2 3 4 ⑤ 6 7
       ance.
    3. has an interest in the age group he/she is coaching.   1 2 ③ 4 5 6 7
    4. respects student's rights.   1 2 ③ 4 5 6 7

Approximate visually or add numbers
and divide by N (i.e., 15 ÷ 4 = 3.75).

instrument is provided to analyze the legal aspects of sports. The manual also includes instruments for evaluating physical education that includes: the physical education curriculum, intramural programs, facilities, and physical education personnel.

All aspects of the physical education program could be assessed using all instruments, or specific programs and personnel could be selected for evaluation on a rotational basis. Whoever is responsible for making this decision can select the appropriate instruments from this manual and apply them to his/her situation to any desired extent.

Occasionally personnel have dual responsibilities. The athletic director may also be the basketball coach, or the head track coach may be the physical education department chairman. In each case, the person should be evaluated in both positions since he/she may be effective in one position, but not in the other. Also, a decision must be made whether a junior varsity coach is to be rated as a head coach or an assistant, and so on.

DEVELOP THE ASSESSMENT PLAN

Once the decision has been made to assess, a plan of action can be formulated as follows:
1. Determine the area(s) to be assessed, i.e., total athletic program, football staff, facilities, etc.
2. Determine who will be the evaluators.
3. Determine who will tabulate the data.
4. Develop a policy as to who should see the results of the evaluations.
5. Establish a due date for returning instruments.
6. Select, type, and distribute the evaluation instruments.
7. Analyze results (see Chapter 3).

8. Make suggestions and a plan of action for improvement.

Additional instructions are provided for assessing the athletic facilities instrument found in Part Three. Directions are different for this evaluation instrument.

Although there are separate instruments for evaluating the head coach and a specific sport, the problem of interaction cannot be ignored. In other words, it would appear difficult to have an outstanding football program with a poor head football coach. On the other hand, it would be possible to have a good head football coach and at the same time have a poor football program (because of a lack of administration support, finances, geographical location, school classification, etc.). The generalization may be made that if one assessment is good, the other will also be good—but that is not necessarily so. For this reason, separate instruments are provided.

It will also be noted that there are a number of items that are duplicated in various assessment instruments. Many traits of the head coach may also apply to an assistant—yet many are also different.

CHAPTER 3

Analyzing the Results of Assessments

A primary reason for assessing programs and personnel is to improve an existing situation. Initially, after going through an assessment program, it might seem desirable to have a final numerical quantity. If that were possible, the final score could be compared with other programs or personnel. Usually such a figure is not a meaningful value, and it appears to be more desirable, when the purpose is to improve what exists, to simply analyze what exists and from that assessment recommend improvements. After changes have been implemented, a subsequent assessment can be made to determine if, in fact, an improvement has occurred. This applies to the total physical education program, which includes the athletic program, any sport, or any personnel involved with the programs. These instruments, then, have their greatest value when analyzing improvement within a program rather than when comparing programs.

A profile analysis is most appropriate for assessment. With a profile, obvious strengths and weaknesses can be identified, and any point on the profile can be compared with subsequent evaluations. The profile analysis gives a quick graphic picture of the total status and, in addition, each subcategory can be examined.

ANALYSIS OF THE ASSESSMENT FORMS

When the assessment forms are distributed, a date should be established as to when the forms are to be returned. On that date, a tally should be made to see that most (preferably all) the forms have been returned. Remember, the more ratings received, the more accurate and unbiased the assessment is likely to be.

Let's assume that ten people were asked to evaluate the head coach and all ten forms have been returned. The next step is to summarize the ratings on a master form. To do this each subcategory (capital letters) of the ten forms should be added and divided by ten to obtain an average rating for each of the subcategories. For example, under I. The Coach in the Profession, A. Professional Preparation, let's assume the ratings were: 5, 6, 4, 5, 6, 5, 4, 5, 4, and 6. This works out to be a mean of 5.0. This point would then be plotted on the profile at I–A. Each additional subcategory can be calculated in the same way. When all five subcategories have been plotted, the mean of the five averages can be obtained for the category rating (see Figure 2).

Figure 2

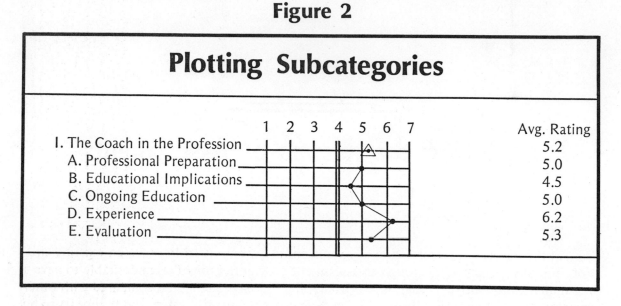

Here, the five subcategories totalled 26.0. Dividing by 5, a rating for the category of The Coach in the Profession is equal to 5.2, well above average, yet noting that there is room for improvement.

This process is continued until all subcategories and categories have been averaged. Although we believe a numerical quantity is of questionable value, each of the main categories could be totalled and averaged for a final numerical rating of the head coach (see Figure 3).

Figure 3

Main Categories for the Assessment Profile of the Head Coach

		Category Rating
I. The Coach in the Profession	1 2 3 4 ⑤ 6 7	5.2
II. The Coach's Knowledge of . . .	1 2 ③ 4 5 6 7	3.1
III. The Coach as a Person	1 2 3 4 5 ⑥ 7	5.7
IV. The Coach as an Organizer	1 ② 3 4 5 6 7	2.1
V. The Coach's Knowledge . . .	1 2 ③ 4 5 6 7	3.3
VI. The Coach and Public Relations	1 2 3 4 ⑤ 6 7	5.0
VII. The Coach's . . .	1 2 3 ④ 5 6 7	3.6
Kinesiological . . .		28.0
	Average Category Rating 28 ÷ 7 =	4.0

Figure 4

Applying Weighted Values

	Category Rating	Weight	Weighted Category
I. The Coach in the Profession	5.2	10	52.0
II. The Coach's Knowledge of . . .	3.1	15	46.5
III. The Coach as a Person	5.7	20	114.0
IV. The Coach as an Organizer	2.1	15	31.5
V. The Coach's Knowledge . . .	3.3	15	49.5
VI. The Coach and Public Relations	5.0	10	50.0
VII. The Coach's . . . kinesiological . . .	3.6	15	54.0
		100	397.5

Thus far we have considered all areas of evaluation of the head coach to be of equal importance. Each item has been equally "weighted." That is, we have said that it is equally important for the head coach to be good in public relations as it is to be a good person or organizer!

As you develop your assessment plans, you may wish to assign different weights to each category. A given school district philosophy, for example, may stress the concept of good public relations, etc. Weights can be assigned to the various categories as shown in Figure 4. For comparison of the composite scores from year to year, these weights must remain constant.

The weights should add up to 100. Since each category has a rating of 1–7, there is a maximum possible weighted score of 700. This maximum possible score is divided into the total Weighted Category Score to get a Composite Score of .57 (397.5 ÷ 700 = .57). This composite score could be used for comparison purposes and to evaluate improvement. A composite score of 1.0 would represent a perfect program or person.

The Category Ratings can also be plotted on the profiles and relative importance established for each category as the profile is inspected. A sample completed Profile for the Intramural Program is shown in Figure 5.

There are three profiles for evaluating athletic facilities—one for middle schools, high schools, and colleges. The profiles are designed somewhat differently and are explained in detail in Part Three.

USE OF THE COMPLETED PROFILE

Once the profile has been completed, it can be analyzed for strengths and weaknesses. Hopefully, the chief school administrator in charge of the assessment will carefully analyze strong as well as weak points—praising those strong points and suggesting improvements on the weak categories.

In the case of the physical education chairperson and the athletic director, the school principal can review the evaluation and thus they can mutually work toward improvement of weak areas. In the case of a specific sport program, the athletic director and coach(es) can review the assessment together and suggest recommendations for improvement. In the case of personnel, the physical education chairperson and the athletic director can review the assessments with respective staff members and make suggestions for improvement.

Assessment forms for personnel can also be used as an aid for considering merit increases in pay and promotions. This is particularly valuable when initial ratings were low and improvement was made on subsequent assessments.

Figure 5

Profile of the Intramural Program (example)

Categories and Subcategories	Subcategory Rating (1 2 3 4 5 6 7)	Category Rating	Weight	Weighted Category
I. Relationship of the Intramural Program to the Total Educational Program		6.0	10	60
A. Purposes and Objectives of the Intramural Program				
II. Fiscal Management		3.5	10	35
A. Revenue/Income				
B. Budget				
C. Equipment				
D. Officials				
III. Relationship of the Intramural Program to the Community		2.0	10	20
A. Public Relations				
IV. Administration of the Intramural Program		5.5	20	110
A. Organization and Planning				
B. Rules and Regulations				
C. Legal Aspects				
D. Intramural Program Curriculum				
E. Personnel				
F. Evaluation Procedures				
V. Facilities for the Intramural Program		6.0	10	60
A. Facilities				
VI. Student in the Intramural Program		4.0	40	160
A. Participation				
B. Health Considerations				
				100

Composite Score:
Sum of Weighted Category ÷ 700 = .64

Average Category Rating:
Sum of 6 Category Ratings ÷ 6 = 4.2

19

The remainder of this chapter includes assessment profiles for each instrument found in the manual.

Profile of the Athletic Director

NAME _____

Categories and Subcategories	Subcategory Rating							Category Rating	Weight	Weighted Category
	1	2	3	4	5	6	7			
I. Fiscal Management										
A. Budget and Finance____										
B. Equipment ____										
C. Transportation____										
D. Officials____										
II. Public Relations										
A. Community____										
B. News Media____										
C. Communication Skills____										
D. Effective Interpersonal Skills____										
III. The Athletic Director in the Profession										
A. Professional Preparation____										
B. Educational Implications____										
C. Ongoing Service____										
D. Experience____										
E. Evaluation____										
IV. The Athletic Director as a Person										
A. Personal Qualities____										
B. Dealings with the Coaching Staff____										
C. Conduct____										
V. The Athletic Director as an Organizer and Administrator										
A. Staff or General____										
B. Game Management____										
C. Purchase and Care of Equipment____										
D. Legal Aspects____										
E. Evaluation____										
F. Recruiting____										
G. Procedural Regulations____										
									100	

Composite Score:
Sum of Weighted Category ÷ 700 = _____

Average Category Rating:
Sum of 5 Category Ratings ÷ 5 = _____

Profile of the Head Coach

NAME _____

Categories and Subcategories	Subcategory Rating							Category Rating	Weight	Weighted Category
	1	2	3	4	5	6	7			
I. The Coach in the Profession										
A. Professional Preparation ____										
B. Educational Implications____										
C. Ongoing Education ____										
D. Experience ____										
E. Self-evaluation ____										
II. The Coach's Knowledge of and Practice of Medical Aspects of Coaching										
A. Preparation of the Athlete for Competition ____										
B. Health and Training Techniques ____										
III. The Coach as a Person										
A. Personal Qualities ____										
B. Dealings with the Team ____										
C. Conduct in Coaching ____										
IV. The Coach as an Organizer and Administrator										
A. Organization of Practice ____										
B. Game Management ____										
C. Purchase and Care of Equipment ____										
D. Finances/Budget____										
E. Legal Aspects ____										
F. Evaluation ____										
G. Recruiting ____										
H. Rules and Regulations ____										
V. The Coach's Knowledge of the Sport										
A. Skills and Techniques and Methods of Coaching ____										
B. Strategies ____										
C. Scouting and Preparation for Opponent ____										
D. Evaluation of Team Personnel ____										
VI. The Coach and Public Relations										
A. Communication Skills ____										
B. News Media ____										
C. Effective Interpersonal Relationships ____										
VII. The Coach's Knowledge of and Application of Kinesiological and Physiological Principles										
A. Movement Analysis____										
B. Growth and Development ____										
C. Nutrition____										
									100	

Composite Score:
Sum of Weighted
Category ÷ 700 = _____

Average Category Rating:
Sum of 7 Category
Ratings ÷ 7 = _____

23

Profile of the Assistant Coach

NAME _____

Categories and Subcategories	Subcategory Rating							Category Rating	Weight	Weighted Category
	1	2	3	4	5	6	7			
I. The Assistant Coach in the Profession										
A. Professional Preparation _____										
B. Educational Implications _____										
C. Ongoing Education _____										
D. Experience _____										
E. Evaluation _____										
II. The Assistant Coach's Knowledge of and Practice of Medical Aspects of Coaching										
A. Preparation of Athlete for Competition _____										
B. Health and Training Techniques _____										
III. The Assistant Coach as a Person										
A. Personal Qualities _____										
B. Dealings with the Team _____										
C. Loyalty to Other Staff Members and Program _____										
D. Conduct in Coaching _____										
IV. General Functions and Responsibilities										
A. Organization of Practice _____										
B. Game Management _____										
C. Purchase and Care of Equipment _____										
D. Legal Aspects _____										
E. Evaluation _____										
F. Recruiting _____										
G. Rules and Regulations _____										
V. The Assistant Coach's Knowledge of the Sport										
A. Skills, Techniques, and Methods of Coaching _____										
B. Strategies _____										
C. Scouting and Preparation for Opponent _____										
D. Evaluation of Team Personnel _____										
VI. The Assistant Coach and Public Relations										
A. Communication Skills _____										
B. News Media _____										
C. Effective Interpersonal Relationships _____										
VII. The Assistant Coach's Knowledge of and Application of Kinesiological and Physiological Principles										
A. Movement Analysis _____										
B. Growth and Development _____										
C. Nutrition _____										
									100	

Composite Score:
Sum of Weighted
Category ÷ 700 = _____

Average Category Rating:
Sum of 7 Category
Ratings ÷ 7 = _____

25

Profile of Officials

NAME _____

CONTEST _____   LOCATION _____

DATE _____

Category	1 2 3 4 5 6 7	Category Rating	Weight	Weighted Category
I. Personal Qualities				
II. Administration of Duties				
III. Mechanics				

Composite Score:
Sum of Weighted
Category ÷ 700 = _____

Average Category Rating:
Sum of 3 Category
Ratings ÷ 3 = _____

27

Profile of the Athletic Trainer

NAME _____

Categories and Subcategories	Subcategory Rating							Category Rating	Weight	Weighted Category
	1	2	3	4	5	6	7			
I. The Trainer in the Profession										
A. Professional Preparation____										
B. Educational Implications ____										
C. Ongoing Education_____										
D. Experience_____										
E. Self-evaluation_____										
II. The Trainer's Knowledge of and Practice of Athletic Training Methods										
A. Preparation of the Athlete for Competition _____										
B. Health and Training Techniques ____										
III. The Trainer as a Person										
A. Personal Qualities_____										
B. Dealings with the Team ____										
C. Loyalty to Staff/Program____										
D. Conduct in Training Program____										
Organization										
IV. General Functions/Responsibilities										
A. Organization _____										
B. Game Management _____										
C. Purchase and Care of Equipment ____										
D. Legal Aspects _____										
E. Evaluation _____										
F. Rules and Regulations _____										
V. The Trainer's Knowledge of Sports										
A. Skills, Techniques, and Methods of Coaching ____										
VI. The Trainer and Public Relations										
A. Communication Skills____										
B. News Media_____										
C. Interpersonal_____										
VII. The Trainer's Knowledge of and Application of Kinesiology and Physiological Principles										
A. Movement Analysis_____										
B. Growth and Development_____										
C. Nutrition_____										

100

Composite Score.
Sum of Weighted
Category ÷ 700 = _____

Average Category Rating:
Sum of 7 Category
Ratings ÷ 7 = _____

29

Profile of the Athletic Program

Categories and Subcategories	Subcategory Rating							Category Rating	Weight	Weighted Category
	1	2	3	4	5	6	7			
I. Relationship of Athletic Program to Total Educational Program										
A. Purposes and Objectives of the Athletic Program										
II. Fiscal Management of the Athletic Program										
A. Revenue/Income										
B. Budget										
C. Equipment										
D. Officials										
III. Relationship of the Athletic Program to the Community										
A. Public Relations										
B. Community										
C. Recruitment of Players										
IV. Administration of Athletic Program										
A. Organization and Planning										
B. Scheduling										
C. Transportation										
D. Personnel										
E. Contest Management										
F. Relations with League and State Associations										
G. Evaluation										
V. Student in the Athletic Program										
A. Participation										
B. School Spirit										
C. Awards										
D. Health Considerations										
E. Student Aid										
F. Relations with League and State Associations										
									100	

Composite Score:
Sum of Weighted
Category ÷ 700 = _____

Average Category Rating:
Sum of 5 Category
Ratings ÷ 5 = _____

Profile of a Sport Program

SPORT _____

Categories and Subcategories	Subcategory Rating							Category Rating	Weight	Weighted Category
	1	2	3	4	5	6	7			
I. Relationship to the Total Educational Program										
A. Goals and Objectives ___										
II. Fiscal Management										
A. Revenue/Income ___										
B. Budget ___										
C. Equipment ___										
D. Officials ___										
III. Relationship to the Community										
A. Public Relations ___										
B. Community ___										
C. Recruitment of Players ___										
IV. Administration of the Program										
A. Organization and Planning ___										
B. Scheduling ___										
C. Transportation ___										
D. Personnel ___										
E. Contest Management ___										
F. Relations with League and State Associations ___										
G. Evaluation ___										
V. Student in the Sport Program										
A. Participation ___										
B. School Spirit ___										
C. Awards ___										
D. Health Considerations ___										
E. Student Aid ___										
										100

Composite Score:
Sum of Weighted
Category ÷ 700 = _____

Average Category Rating
Sum of 5 Category
Ratings ÷ 5 = _____

33

Profile of Legal Aspects in Sports

Categories and Subcategories	Subcategory Rating							Category Rating	Weight	Weighted Category
	1	2	3	4	5	6	7			
I. General Liability										
A. Insurance										
B. Classification and Association Relations										
C. Standard of Care										
D. Transportation										
E. Spectators										
F. Supervision										
G. Miscellaneous										
II. Equipment and Facilities										
A. Equipment										
B. Facilities										
III. Medical Aspects										
A. Legal Considerations— Preseason										
B. Legal Considerations— During Seasons										
C. Legal Considerations— Postcontest or Postseason										
IV. Records and Information on Athletes										
A. Health Records										
B. Documents from Parents										
C. Assessment of Performance										

100

Average Category Rating:
Sum of 4 Category
Ratings ÷ 4 = _____

Composite Score:
Sum of Weighted
Category ÷ 700 = _____

Profile of the
Physical Education Department Chairperson

NAME _____

Categories and Subcategories	Subcategory Rating							Category Rating	Weight	Weighted Category
	1	2	3	4	5	6	7			
I. Personal Qualities										
A. Human Relations										
B. Personality Traits										
C. Physical Characteristics										
II. Professional Growth										
A. Personal Reading and Writing										
B. Affiliation with Professional Associations										
C. Professional Interaction										
III. Administrative Responsibilities										
A. Organization										
B. Communication Skills										
C. Leadership										
D. Staff Relationships										
E. Planning and Foresight										
F. Daily Operation										
G. Decision-making Abilities										
H. Problem-solving Abilities										

100

Average Category Rating:
Sum of 3 Category
Ratings ÷ 3 =   _____

Composite Score:
Sum of Weighted
Category ÷ 700 =   _____

Profile of the Physical Educator

NAME _____

Categories and Subcategories	Subcategory Rating							Category Rating	Weight	Weighted Category
	1	2	3	4	5	6	7			
I. The Teacher in the Profession										
A. Professional Preparation										
B. Educational Implications										
C. Ongoing Education										
D. Personal Evaluation										
II. Instructional Responsibilities										
A. Class Management										
B. Instructional Skills										
C. Knowledge of Subject Matter										
D. Discipline										
E. Attendance										
III. Personal Qualities										
A. Human Relations										
B. Personality Traits										
C. Physical Characteristics										
IV. Public Relations										
A. Communication Skills										
B. Interpersonal Relations										

100

Average Category Rating:
Sum of 4 Category
Ratings ÷ 4 = _____

Composite Score:
Sum of Weighted
Category ÷ 700 = _____

Profile of the Physical Education Program

Categories and Subcategories	Subcategory Rating							Category Rating	Weight	Weighted Category
	1	2	3	4	5	6	7			
I. Relationship of Physical Education Program to Total Educational Program										
A. Purposes and Objectives of the Physical Education Program _____										
II. Fiscal Management of the Physical Education Program										
A. Budget _____										
B. Equipment _____										
III. Relationship of Physical Education Program to the Community										
A. Public Relations _____										
B. Community _____										
IV. Administration of the Physical Education Program										
A. Organization _____										
B. Personnel _____										
C. Evaluation _____										
V. The Curriculum in the Physical Education Program										
A. Course of Study _____										
VI. Student in the Physical Education Program										
A. Participation _____										
									100	

Average Category Rating:
Sum of 6 Category
Ratings ÷ 6 = _____

Composite Score:
Sum of Weighted
Category ÷ 700 = _____

41

Profile of the Intramural Program

Categories and Subcategories	Subcategory Rating							Category Rating	Weight	Weighted Category
	1	2	3	4	5	6	7			
I. Relationship of the Intramural Program to the Total Educational Program										
A. Purposes and Objectives of the Intramural Program										
II. Fiscal Management										
A. Revenue/Income										
B. Budget										
C. Equipment										
D. Officials										
III. Relationship of the Intramural Program to the Community										
A. Public Relations										
IV. Administration of the Intramural Program										
A. Organization and Planning										
B. Rules and Regulations										
C. Legal Aspects										
D. Intramural Program Curriculum										
E. Personnel										
F. Evaluation Procedures										
V. Facilities for the Intramural Program										
A. Facilities										
VI. Student in the Intramural Program										
A. Participation										
B. Health Considerations										
									100	

Composite Score:
Sum of Weighted
Category ÷ 700 = _____

Average Category Rating:
Sum of 6 Category
Ratings ÷ 6 = _____

43

Athletic Facility Profile–Middle School

10	20	30	40	50	60	70	80	90	Description	Area
									Athletic Office	1
									Athletic Locker Room	2
									Athletic Shower Room	3
									Training Room	4
									Weight-training Room	5
									Athletic Storage	6
									Laundry and Drying Area	7
									Main Gymnasium	8
									Baseball and Softball	9
									Football Field	10
									Track and Field	11
									Tennis Courts	12
									Aquatics	13

45

Athletic Facility Profile–High School

	Description	Area
	Athletic Office	1
	Athletic Locker Room	2
	Athletic Shower Room	3
	Training Room	4
	Weight-training Room	5
	Athletic Storage	6
	Laundry and Drying Area	7
	Main Gymnasium	8
	Baseball and Softball	9
	Football Field	10
	Track and Field	11
	Tennis Courts	12
	Aquatics	13

Scale across top: 10 20 30 40 50 60 70 80 90

47

Athletic Facility Profile–Community College

10 20 30 40 50 60 70 80 90	Description	Area
	Athletic Office	1
	Athletic Locker Room	2
	Athletic Shower Room	3
	Training Room	4
	Weight-training Room	5
	Athletic Storage	6
	Laundry and Drying Area	7
	Main Gymnasium	8
	Baseball and Softball	9
	Football Field	10
	Track and Field	11
	Tennis Courts	12
	Aquatics	13

49

PART TWO

Athletic Personnel Assessment Instruments

Directions for Evaluating the Athletic Director

ATHLETIC DIRECTOR _____

    This evaluation instrument consists of five major categories that are identified by Roman numerals. Within each major category there are varying numbers of subcategories that are identified by capital letters. *These are the ratings we are interested in.* To the right of each subcategory heading you will find a scale from 1–7. After you have examined the statements listed under each subcategory, circle the number for the subcategory that best represents your opinion of that area. The numerous statements (listed by Arabic numerals) are used merely as an aid to help you make a better evaluation of the subcategory rating. These statements also have the 1–7 scale; in addition, some may be answered NO or YES (if the response is NO circle 1, if the response is YES circle 7). The individual statements ratings can be "eyeballed" to determine the subcategory rating or the statements rated can be added and divided by the number of items rated (N) to determine an average subcategory rating. There may be statements that *do not apply* to your situation or *demand information not available* to you. If this is true simply *omit responding* to those items. Add any additional comments in the left-hand margin.

EXAMPLE:

III. The Athletic Director in the Profession

    A. Professional Preparation   1   2   ③   4   5   6   7
Comments
    The athletic director:
    1. is a certified teacher.   1   2   3   4   5   6   ⑦
    2. has a background in physical education.   1   ②   3   4   5   6   7
    3. has a background in athletics.   1   2   3   4   ⑤   6   7
    4. has had courses in organization   ?   1   2   3   4   5   6   7
       and administration.

                                 Approximate visually or add numbers
                                   and divide by N for subcategory rating
                                   (i.e., $14 \div 3 = 4.7$).

Assessment of the Athletic Director

I. Fiscal Management

A. Budget and Finance   1 2 3 4 5 6 7
Comments

The athletic director makes certain:

1. there is a written policy governing the revenue and expenditures of funds for athletics.   1 2 3 4 5 6 7
2. financial policies governing athletics are made known to all coaches.   1 2 3 4 5 6 7
3. a yearly itemized athletic budget is prepared.   1 2 3 4 5 6 7
4. all involved coaches are allowed input into the budgetary process.   1 2 3 4 5 6 7
5. there is an equitable distribution of funds to all sports in the program.   1 2 3 4 5 6 7
6. a completed budget is available for the use of all coaches.   1 2 3 4 5 6 7
7. up-to-date financial records are kept during the year.   1 2 3 4 5 6 7
8. records of past years are kept for purposes of evaluation and future planning.   1 2 3 4 5 6 7
9. there is a written policy regarding accountability of coaches for athletic budgets.   1 2 3 4 5 6 7
10. the administration is kept informed on expenditures and income of the athletic program.   1 2 3 4 5 6 7
11. there is accountability for income revenues.   1 2 3 4 5 6 7
12. special fund-raising projects are approved in advance.   1 2 3 4 5 6 7
13. monthly and annual budgetary reports are distributed to appropriate administrators and coaches.   1 2 3 4 5 6 7
14. each coach stays within the budget.   1 2 3 4 5 6 7
15. he/she assists in raising supplementary funds.   1 2 3 4 5 6 7

B. Equipment   1 2 3 4 5 6 7
Comments

The athletic director makes certain:

1. proper procedures for purchasing equipment and supplies are used.   1 2 3 4 5 6 7
2. equipment and supplies are properly chosen and ordered.   1 2 3 4 5 6 7
3. long-range planning is done to provide for replacement and purchase of major equipment items.   1 2 3 4 5 6 7

C. Transportation   1 2 3 4 5 6 7
Comments

The athletic director makes certain:

55

(continued on the next page)

    1. there is a clearly written policy for the request of transportation.   1 2 3 4 5 6 7

    2. this policy is known by all coaches.   1 2 3 4 5 6 7

    3. there is a clearly written policy regarding the type of transportation that may be used in athletics.   1 2 3 4 5 6 7

    4. the transportation policy is known by all involved coaches.   1 2 3 4 5 6 7

    5. all transportation requests are checked.   1 2 3 4 5 6 7

  D. Officials   1 2 3 4 5 6 7

Comments

    The athletic director makes certain:

    1. all officials are contacted and contracted for all home contests.   1 2 3 4 5 6 7

    2. officials are paid at the proper time/rate/etc.   1 2 3 4 5 6 7

    3. adequate facilities are ready for officials (dressing room, access to showers, towels).   1 2 3 4 5 6 7

    4. properly qualified and certified officials are obtained for all contests.   1 2 3 4 5 6 7

    5. proper security procedures are taken for safeguarding officials.   1 2 3 4 5 6 7

II. Public Relations

  A. Community   1 2 3 4 5 6 7

Comments

    The athletic director makes certain:

    1. parents are informed in writing of school athletic policies concerning trip arrangements, insurance programs, code of conduct, etc.   1 2 3 4 5 6 7

    2. the community is informed of major changes in the athletic program.   1 2 3 4 5 6 7

    3. all sporting events are publicized (dates of contests, time of contest).   1 2 3 4 5 6 7

    4. that good relations with booster clubs and service clubs are maintained.   1 2 3 4 5 6 7

    5. that scheduled contests do not conflict with community activities.   1 2 3 4 5 6 7

  B. News Media   1 2 3 4 5 6 7

Comments

    The athletic director:

    1. understands the importance of good relations with the news media.   1 2 3 4 5 6 7

    2. cooperates with the news media.   1 2 3 4 5 6 7

    3. encourages the various coaches to cooperate with the news media.   1 2 3 4 5 6 7

    4. communicates effectively with the news media.   1 2 3 4 5 6 7

(*continued on the next page*)

5. educates the coaches in understanding the importance of good relations with the news media. 1 2 3 4 5 6 7

6. encourages the news media to participate in the program (provision of season passes, facilities at games, etc.). 1 2 3 4 5 6 7

C. Communication Skills 1 2 3 4 5 6 7

Comments

The athletic director:

1. is articulate. 1 2 3 4 5 6 7
2. uses good grammar. 1 2 3 4 5 6 7
3. has good writing skills. 1 2 3 4 5 6 7

D. Effective Interpersonal Skills 1 2 3 4 5 6 7

Comments

The athletic director:

1. has good rapport with the administration of the school. 1 2 3 4 5 6 7
2. fairly represents the coaches and their problems to the administration. 1 2 3 4 5 6 7
3. maintains an open and democratic relationship with the coaching staff. 1 2 3 4 5 6 7
4. cooperates with the student body. 1 2 3 4 5 6 7
5. maintains effective communication and relationship with league members. 1 2 3 4 5 6 7
6. maintains an open and cooperative spirit with the faculty. 1 2 3 4 5 6 7

III. The Athletic Director in the Profession

A. Professional Preparation 1 2 3 4 5 6 7

Comments

The athletic director:

1. is a certified teacher. 1 2 3 4 5 6 7
2. has a background in physical education. 1 2 3 4 5 6 7
3. has a background in athletics. 1 2 3 4 5 6 7
4. has had courses in organization and administration. 1 2 3 4 5 6 7
5. has had courses in business and management. 1 2 3 4 5 6 7
6. has had courses in personnel or human relations. 1 2 3 4 5 6 7

B. Educational Implications 1 2 3 4 5 6 7

Comments

The athletic director:

1. understands the role of athletics in education. 1 2 3 4 5 6 7
2. knows the objectives of the athletic program. 1 2 3 4 5 6 7
3. assists in defining the objectives of the athletic program to the school, staff, community, etc. 1 2 3 4 5 6 7
4. assists in formulating new objectives or bringing old objectives up-to-date. 1 2 3 4 5 6 7

(continued on the next page)

5. has a sound philosophy of athletics.	1	2	3	4	5	6	7
6. performs his/her function as a faculty person.	1	2	3	4	5	6	7
C. Ongoing Service	1	2	3	4	5	6	7

Comments

The athletic director:

1. has attended clinic(s), workshop(s), seminar(s) or taken courses relating to athletic administration in the last three years.	1	2	3	4	5	6	7
2. is an active member of any professional associations relating to athletic administration.	1	2	3	4	5	6	7
3. subscribes to appropriate professional journals relating to athletic administration.	1	2	3	4	5	6	7
D. Experience	1	2	3	4	5	6	7

Comments

The athletic director:

1. participated as a player in an athletic sport.	1	2	3	4	5	6	7
2. has had experience as a head coach in a sport.	1	2	3	4	5	6	7
3. has had administrative experience.	1	2	3	4	5	6	7
E. Evaluation	1	2	3	4	5	6	7

Comments

The athletic director:

1. does a thorough self-evaluation each year on his/her administrative ability and expertise.	1	2	3	4	5	6	7
2. has others (administration and coaches) evaluate his/her performance as an athletic director each year.	1	2	3	4	5	6	7

IV. The Athletic Director as a Person

A. Personal Qualities	1	2	3	4	5	6	7

Comments

The athletic director:

1. has high moral values.	1	2	3	4	5	6	7
2. sets a positive example in word, deed, and appearance (to staff and athletes).	1	2	3	4	5	6	7
3. has an interest in the age group of the athletes in the program he/she is directing.	1	2	3	4	5	6	7
4. believes in coach's rights.	1	2	3	4	5	6	7
5. believes in students' rights.	1	2	3	4	5	6	7
6. has a positive attitude and enthusiastic personality.	1	2	3	4	5	6	7
7. has emotional stability and self-control.	1	2	3	4	5	6	7
8. is flexible and adaptable in his/her attitude toward youth and societal changes.	1	2	3	4	5	6	7
9. possesses personality traits that indicate he/she is a secure person.	1	2	3	4	5	6	7
10. keeps physically fit.	1	2	3	4	5	6	7
11. is an effective leader.	1	2	3	4	5	6	7

61

(continued on the next page)

B. Dealings with the Coaching Staff   1 2 3 4 5 6 7
Comments

The athletic director:

1. maintains an open and democratic relationship with the coaching staff.   1 2 3 4 5 6 7
2. helps the coaching staff.   1 2 3 4 5 6 7
3. keeps coaches informed of changes in rules and regulations.   1 2 3 4 5 6 7
4. keeps coaches informed of acceptable and nonacceptable dress and grooming codes for the staff.   1 2 3 4 5 6 7
5. is fair and equitable to all sports in the program.   1 2 3 4 5 6 7
6. is capable of giving effective counsel to coaches.   1 2 3 4 5 6 7
7. recognizes and respects individual differences in coaches.   1 2 3 4 5 6 7
8. supports the coaches and helps them grow professionally.   1 2 3 4 5 6 7

C. Conduct   1 2 3 4 5 6 7
Comments

The athletic director:

1. encourages good sportsmanship in coaches.   1 2 3 4 5 6 7
2. is ethical and respectful in conduct toward opponents.   1 2 3 4 5 6 7
3. is ethical and respectful in conduct toward officials.   1 2 3 4 5 6 7
4. is understanding and respectful to parents.   1 2 3 4 5 6 7
5. places the importance of the athlete above winning.   1 2 3 4 5 6 7
6. keeps winning in its appropriate perspective In relation to the total objective of the program.   1 2 3 4 5 6 7

V. The Athletic Director as an Organizer and Administrator

A. Staff or General   1 2 3 4 5 6 7
Comments

The athletic director makes certain:

1. the objectives of the athletic program are thoroughly and clearly written out.   1 2 3 4 5 6 7
2. the objectives of the athletic program are known by all coaches.   1 2 3 4 5 6 7
3. practice facilities are regularly checked and maintained.   1 2 3 4 5 6 7
4. game facilities are regularly checked and maintained.   1 2 3 4 5 6 7
5. practice facilities are scheduled in a fair and equitable method.   1 2 3 4 5 6 7
6. all policies and procedures governing athletics are thoroughly and clearly written.   1 2 3 4 5 6 7
7. that the coaches know all policies and procedures governing athletics.   1 2 3 4 5 6 7

(continued on the next page)

8. policy or procedural changes are clearly written.	1	2	3	4	5	6	7
9. policy and procedural changes are made known to all coaches.	1	2	3	4	5	6	7
10. weekly/monthly staff meetings are held to develop policy and resolve problems.	1	2	3	4	5	6	7
11. the scheduling of events is conducted in order to maintain maximum utilization of existing facilities.	1	2	3	4	5	6	7
12. the school is properly represented in the organization and planning of league business.	1	2	3	4	5	6	7

B. Game Management   1 2 3 4 5 6 7

Comments

The athletic director makes certain:

1. that proper game management is understood and planned for effectively.	1	2	3	4	5	6	7
2. playing facilities and equipment are ready.	1	2	3	4	5	6	7
3. the visiting team is properly accommodated (locker room ready, towels, parking of bus, etc.).	1	2	3	4	5	6	7
4. that arrangements and accommodations for officials are ready.	1	2	3	4	5	6	7
5. that financial arrangements for officials are proper.	1	2	3	4	5	6	7
6. that arrangements for timers, scorers, ticket sellers and takers, news media and/or other personnel are handled effectively.	1	2	3	4	5	6	7
7. that effective crowd control methods or arrangements are used.	1	2	3	4	5	6	7
8. that crowd accommodations are prepared in advance.	1	2	3	4	5	6	7
9. there are arrangements for emergency first aid procedures at contests.	1	2	3	4	5	6	7
10. that there are clearly written transportation policies and procedures.	1	2	3	4	5	6	7
11. that the coaches know the policies and procedures regarding transportation.	1	2	3	4	5	6	7
12. all policies and procedures for nonhome contests are thoroughly and clearly written.	1	2	3	4	5	6	7
13. all coaches know the policies and procedures for nonhome contests.	1	2	3	4	5	6	7
14. all game contracts are handled effectively.	1	2	3	4	5	6	7
15. all game contracts are available on request or need.	1	2	3	4	5	6	7
16. that postgame responsibilities are planned and handled effectively.	1	2	3	4	5	6	7
17. an effective checklist for game management is established.	1	2	3	4	5	6	7
18. that precontest activities/ceremonies are appropriate and are managed effectively.	1	2	3	4	5	6	7
19. that intermission activities are appropriate and managed effectively.	1	2	3	4	5	6	7

65

(continued on the next page)

C. Purchase and Care of Equipment   1 2 3 4 5 6 7
Comments

The athletic director:
1. has clearly written policies and procedures for purchasing equipment.   1 2 3 4 5 6 7
2. makes certain that all coaches know the written policies and procedures for purchasing equipment.   1 2 3 4 5 6 7
3. knows the process of how to purchase equipment by bidding.   1 2 3 4 5 6 7
4. makes certain that effective ways to mark and identify equipment are used.   1 2 3 4 5 6 7
5. keeps effective equipment records and inventories.   1 2 3 4 5 6 7
6. makes certain that effective methods for properly caring for equipment are used.   1 2 3 4 5 6 7

D. Legal Aspects   1 2 3 4 5 6 7
Comments

The athletic director:
1. knows what constitutes liability.   1 2 3 4 5 6 7
2. understands the concept of negligence.   1 2 3 4 5 6 7
3. makes certain that the coaches know what constitutes liability.   1 2 3 4 5 6 7
4. makes certain all coaches know and understand the concept of negligence.   1 2 3 4 5 6 7
5. makes certain there is a thorough and clearly written policy on the proper procedure to be taken whenever an injury occurs.   1 2 3 4 5 6 7
6. makes certain all coaches know and follow proper procedures whenever an injury occurs.   1 2 3 4 5 6 7
7. makes certain that coaches are not doing questionable practices that might make the coach liable (supplying pills, vitamins, aspirin, playing athletes with injuries, etc.).   1 2 3 4 5 6 7
8. encourages all coaches to be reasonable and prudent in their conduct.   1 2 3 4 5 6 7
9. makes certain coaches know how to avoid damage suits through preventive measures.   1 2 3 4 5 6 7
10. makes certain that coaches require written permission slips from parents before a student may turn out for a sport.   1 2 3 4 5 6 7
11. makes certain all players have some form of insurance.   1 2 3 4 5 6 7
12. makes certain coaches know of the various types of insurance available to them.   1 2 3 4 5 6 7
13. makes certain that safe facilities are provided and maintained for all athletes.   1 2 3 4 5 6 7
14. is aware of all aspects of legally transporting athletes and related groups to contests.   1 2 3 4 5 6 7

(continued on the next page)

15. helps in planning effective ways to prevent injuries to and lawsuits by spectators.　　1　2　3　4　5　6　7
16. is aware of and adheres to the rules and regulations of state and national associations.　　1　2　3　4　5　6　7
17. makes certain that all athletes in all sports have pre-season physical examinations.　　1　2　3　4　5　6　7

E. Evaluation　　1　2　3　4　5　6　7
Comments

The athletic director:
1. effectively evaluates the progress of the total athletic program annually.　　1　2　3　4　5　6　7
2. effectively evaluates the progress of each sport in the athletic program periodically.　　1　2　3　4　5　6　7
3. effectively evaluates each coach in the athletic program annually.　　1　2　3　4　5　6　7
4. keeps the administration informed on the athletic program (total, each sport, coaches).　　1　2　3　4　5　6　7
5. keeps the administration informed on changing goals or objectives of the program.　　1　2　3　4　5　6　7
6. helps to evaluate officials in an objective manner.　　1　2　3　4　5　6　7
7. evaluates facilities periodically.　　1　2　3　4　5　6　7
8. initiates and plans for future facility needs.　　1　2　3　4　5　6　7

F. Recruiting　　1　2　3　4　5　6　7
Comments

The athletic director:
1. assists the coaches in formulating effective recruiting plans.　　1　2　3　4　5　6　7
2. assists coaches in recruiting.　　1　2　3　4　5　6　7
3. makes certain recruiting regulations are not violated.　　1　2　3　4　5　6　7

G. Procedural Regulations　　1　2　3　4　5　6　7
Comments

The athletic director makes certain:
1. all athletes are informed about the school rules and regulations governing athletics.　　1　2　3　4　5　6　7
2. all athletes are informed about district rules and regulations governing athletics.　　1　2　3　4　5　6　7
3. all coaches are informed of school regulations governing athletics.　　1　2　3　4　5　6　7
4. all coaches are informed of district/state regulations governing athletics.　　1　2　3　4　5　6　7
5. all coaches have a copy of the state handbook.　　1　2　3　4　5　6　7
6. all coaches know state rules and regulation governing athletics.　　1　2　3　4　5　6　7
7. each coach has the national rule book for his/her sport.　　1　2　3　4　5　6　7
8. all coaches are aware of his/her procedural rights.　　1　2　3　4　5　6　7
9. that student athletes know their procedural rights.　　1　2　3　4　5　6　7
10. all coaches enforce all rules and regulations (school, league, state, national).　　1　2　3　4　5　6　7

69

Directions for Evaluating the Head Coach

COACH _____   SPORT _____

This evaluation instrument consists of seven major categories that are identified by Roman numerals. Within each major category there are varying numbers of subcategories that are identified by capital letters. *These are the ratings we are interested in.* To the right of each subcategory heading you will find a scale from 1-7. After you have examined the statements listed under each subcategory, circle the number for the subcategory that best represents your opinion of that area. The numerous statements (listed by Arabic numerals) are used merely as an aid to help you make a better evaluation of the subcategory rating. These statements also have the 1-7 scale; in addition, some may be answered NO or YES (if the response is NO circle 1, if the response is YES circle 7). The individual statements ratings can be "eyeballed" to determine the subcategory rating or the statements rated can be added and divided by the number of items rated (N) to determine an average subcategory rating. There may be statements that *do not apply* to your situation or *demand information not available* to you. If this is true simply *omit responding* to those items. Add any additional comments in the left-hand margin.

EXAMPLE:

III. The Coach as a Person

A. Personal Qualities	1 2 3 ④ 5 6 7
Comments	
The coach:	
1. has high moral values.	1 2 3 ④ 5 6 7
2. sets a positive example in word, deed, and appearance.	1 2 3 4 ⑤ 6 7
3. has an interest in the age group he/she is working with.	1 2 ③ 4 5 6 7
4. respects students rights.	1 2 ③ 4 5 6 7

Approximate visually or add numbers and divide by N for subcategory rating (i.e., $15 \div 4 = 3.75$).

Assessment of the Head Coach

I. The Coach in the Profession

A. Professional Preparation   1   2   3   4   5   6   7

Comments

The coach:

1. is a certified teacher.	1	2	3	4	5	6	7
2. has an undergraduate degree major in physical education or a minor in coaching.	1	2	3	4	5	6	7
3. has taken a course(s) in theory of coaching in the sport.	1	2	3	4	5	6	7
4. has taken a course(s) in fundamentals (techniques) of coaching in the sport.	1	2	3	4	5	6	7
5. has taken a course(s) in safety and first aid.	1	2	3	4	5	6	7
6. has taken a course(s) in care and prevention of athletic injuries.	1	2	3	4	5	6	7
7. has taken a course(s) in officiating in the sport he/she is coaching.	1	2	3	4	5	6	7

B. Educational Implications   1   2   3   4   5   6   7

Comments

The coach:

1. understands the role of athletics in education.	1	2	3	4	5	6	7
2. knows the objectives of the athletic program.	1	2	3	4	5	6	7
3. has a coaching philosophy that is in accordance with the objectives of the athletic program.	1	2	3	4	5	6	7
4. effectively functions as a faculty person.	1	2	3	4	5	6	7

C. Ongoing Education   1   2   3   4   5   6   7

Comments

The coach:

1. has attended a clinic(s), workshop(s), seminar(s) or taken courses relating to athletic coaching in the last five years.	1	2	3	4	5	6	7
2. is an active member of professional associations relating to athletic coaching.	1	2	3	4	5	6	7
3. subscribes to professional journals relating to athletic coaching.	1	2	3	4	5	6	7

D. Experience   1   2   3   4   5   6   7

Comments

The coach:

1. participated as a player in the sport.	1	2	3	4	5	6	7
2. has had experience in coaching the sport as an undergraduate (practicum in coaching, laboratory, student teaching).	1	2	3	4	5	6	7
3. has been an assistant coach in the sport.	1	2	3	4	5	6	7
4. has been a head coach in the sport.	1	2	3	4	5	6	7

(continued on the next page)

E. Self-evaluation	1	2	3	4	5	6	7

Comments

The coach:

1. does an annual self-evaluation on his/her coaching ability and expertise.	1	2	3	4	5	6	7
2. is evaluated by others (athletic director, principal, staff, players, etc.) annually.	1	2	3	4	5	6	7

II. The Coach's Knowledge of and Practice of Medical Aspects of Coaching

A. Preparation of the Athlete for Competition	1	2	3	4	5	6	7

Comments

The coach:

1. makes certain that all players have a physical examination before turning out for a sport.	1	2	3	4	5	6	7
2. understands early season conditioning of athletes.	1	2	3	4	5	6	7
3. is knowledgeable about the factors related to exercise such as:	1	2	3	4	5	6	7
a. fluid balance in the body (use of water in practice and games, use of salt tablets, etc.).	1	2	3	4	5	6	7
b. environmental influences relating to body temperatures (heat, cold, humidity, and altitude).	1	2	3	4	5	6	7
c. limits imposed upon athletes with normal hearts.	1	2	3	4	5	6	7
d. oxygen debt.	1	2	3	4	5	6	7
e. hyperventilation.	1	2	3	4	5	6	7
4. keeps up-to-date medical records on each player.	1	2	3	4	5	6	7
B. Health and Training Techniques	1	2	3	4	5	6	7

Comments

The coach:

1. is knowledgeable about good general health habits (showers, clean uniforms and undergarments in practice and contests, grooming, not drinking from the same containers, etc.).	1	2	3	4	5	6	7
2. knows the latest methods of taping.	1	2	3	4	5	6	7
3. knows how to properly use training room equipment.	1	2	3	4	5	6	7
4. uses proper measures for prevention of injuries.	1	2	3	4	5	6	7
5. is knowledgeable about emergency care of injuries.	1	2	3	4	5	6	7
6. is knowledgeable about proper postinjury care and rehabilitation.	1	2	3	4	5	6	7
7. requires written permission by a physician for an injured athlete to report back for competition.	1	2	3	4	5	6	7
8. is knowledgeable about how to counsel an injured athlete.	1	2	3	4	5	6	7
9. institutes proper training rules that are enforceable.	1	2	3	4	5	6	7

(*continued on the next page*)

10. is knowledgeable about training and conditioning athletes throughout a season (retain conditioning, avoid staleness, etc.). 1 2 3 4 5 6 7

11. provides for someone to properly fit equipment in order to prevent injuries. 1 2 3 4 5 6 7

III. The Coach as a Person

A. Personal Qualities 1 2 3 4 5 6 7

Comments

The coach:

1. has high moral values. 1 2 3 4 5 6 7
2. sets a positive example in word, deed, and appearance.
3. has an interest in the age group he/she is coaching. 1 2 3 4 5 6 7
4. respects students rights. 1 2 3 4 5 6
5. has a positive attitude and enthusiastic personality. 1 2 3 4 5 6 7
6. has emotional stability and self-control. 1 2 3 4 5 6 7
7. is flexible in his/her attitude toward youth and societal changes. 1 2 3 4 5 6 7
8. is a good public speaker. 1 2 3 4 5 6 7
9. cooperates with school staff, parents, and community. 1 2 3 4 5 6 7
10. keeps physically fit. 1 2 3 4 5 6 7
11. knows how to motivate athletes. 1 2 3 4 5 6 7
12. is an effective leader. 1 2 3 4 5 6 7
13. is the kind of person the players can "look up to." 1 2 3 4 5 6 7

B. Dealings with the Team 1 2 3 4 5 6 7

Comments

The coach:

1. is fair and consistent in discipline. 1 2 3 4 5 6 7
2. makes certain the athletes know the training rules and other rules and requirements (such as grooming, eligibility, etc.). 1 2 3 4 5 6 7
3. makes certain the athletes know the consequences of breaking training rules and other rules and requirements. 1 2 3 4 5 6 7
4. is fair in selecting teams. 1 2 3 4 5 6 7
5. is effective in selecting teams. 1 2 3 4 5 6 7
6. is honest in dealing with athletes. 1 2 3 4 5 6 7
7. is approachable to players. 1 2 3 4 5 6 7
8. uses effective guidance techniques. 1 2 3 4 5 6 7
9. respects individual differences in players. 1 2 3 4 5 6 7
10. is concerned about athletes' academic achievements. 1 2 3 4 5 6 7

(continued on the next page)

C. Conduct in Coaching   1 2 3 4 5 6 7
Comments

The coach:

1. demonstrates good sportsmanship. 1 2 3 4 5 6 7
2. teaches good sportsmanship to players. 1 2 3 4 5 6 7
3. is respectful toward opponents. 1 2 3 4 5 6 7
4. is respectful toward officials. 1 2 3 4 5 6 7
5. is respectful and cooperative with news media personnel. 1 2 3 4 5 6 7
6. is understanding and respectful with parents. 1 2 3 4 5 6 7
7. places the importance of the athlete above winning. 1 2 3 4 5 6 7
8. would not sacrifice or compromise personal values or principles "to win." 1 2 3 4 5 6 7
9. supports assistants and helps them to grow professionally. 1 2 3 4 5 6 7
10. supports other sports in the program. 1 2 3 4 5 6 7
11. supports other coaches in the program. 1 2 3 4 5 6 7

IV. The Coach as an Organizer and Administrator

A. Organization or Practice   1 2 3 4 5 6 7
Comments

The coach:

1. effectively plans daily practices. 1 2 3 4 5 6 7
2. posts daily practice schedules. 1 2 3 4 5 6 7
3. plans for effective use of facilities and equipment. 1 2 3 4 5 6 7
4. uses the staff effectively. 1 2 3 4 5 6 7
5. uses the staff in planning practice sessions. 1 2 3 4 5 6 7
6. delegates responsibility effectively. 1 2 3 4 5 6 7
7. employs democratic and fair practices in scheduling facilities for practices. 1 2 3 4 5 6 7

B. Game Management   1 2 3 4 5 6 7
Comments

The coach:

1. plans game management effectively. 1 2 3 4 5 6 7
2. makes certain playing facilities and equipment are ready for game contests. 1 2 3 4 5 6 7
3. makes certain the visiting team is properly accommodated (locker room, towels, etc.). 1 2 3 4 5 6 7
4. makes certain all crowd accommodations are in readiness. 1 2 3 4 5 6 7
5. makes certain that accommodations for officials are in readiness. 1 2 3 4 5 6 7
6. has arrangements made for the timers, scorers, etc. 1 2 3 4 5 6 7

79

(continued on the next page)

7. makes certain emergency first aid procedures are provided (physician in attendance and an ambulance when needed).	1 2 3 4 5 6 7
8. prepares for nonhome contests effectively (transportation, meals, etc.).	1 2 3 4 5 6 7
9. has contracts on all games available.	1 2 3 4 5 6 7
10. keeps player eligibility lists up-to-date for each contest.	1 2 3 4 5 6 7
11. makes certain accommodations for news media are in readiness.	1 2 3 4 5 6 7
12. takes care of postgame responsibilities effectively.	1 2 3 4 5 6 7
C. Purchase and Care of Equipment	1 2 3 4 5 6 7

Comments

The coach:

1. follows proper methods (policy of the school) in purchasing equipment.	1 2 3 4 5 6 7
2. uses effective ways to mark and identify equipment.	1 2 3 4 5 6 7
3. keeps up-to-date equipment and inventory records.	1 2 3 4 5 6 7
D. Finances/Budget	1 2 3 4 5 6 7

Comments

The coach:

1. understands the finances/budget of the program.	1 2 3 4 5 6 7
2. operates as efficiently as possible on the allowed budget.	1 2 3 4 5 6 7
3. stays within the allotted budget.	1 2 3 4 5 6 7
4. understands the proper place and use of supplemental funds in the budget.	1 2 3 4 5 6 7
E. Legal Aspects	1 2 3 4 5 6 7

Comments

The coach:

1. knows what constitutes liability.	1 2 3 4 5 6 7
2. understands the concept of negligence.	1 2 3 4 5 6 7
3. knows the proper procedures to be taken when an injury occurs.	1 2 3 4 5 6 7
4. knows questionable practices that might make him/her liable (supply pills, aspirin, anticold, vitamin C, permitting players to play with an injury, etc.).	1 2 3 4 5 6 7
5. employs reasonable and prudent conduct.	1 2 3 4 5 6 7
6. knows how to avoid damage suits through preventive measures.	1 2 3 4 5 6 7
7. requires written permission slips from parents before a student may turn out for a sport.	1 2 3 4 5 6 7
F. Evaluation	1 2 3 4 5 6 7

Comments

The coach:

1. periodically evaluates the progress of the program.	1 2 3 4 5 6 7
2. keeps the administration informed about the program.	1 2 3 4 5 6 7

81

(continued on the next page)

	1	2	3	4	5	6	7
3. evaluates the staff effectively (assistants, managers).	1	2	3	4	5	6	7
4. evaluates officials effectively.	1	2	3	4	5	6	7
G. Recruiting (In programs requiring this area)	1	2	3	4	5	6	7

Comments

The coach:

	1	2	3	4	5	6	7
1. has the necessary personality to recruit effectively.	1	2	3	4	5	6	7
2. effectively plans the use of budgeted monies for recruiting.	1	2	3	4	5	6	7
3. has a systematic means of recruiting athletes from lower level schools that feed into the program.	1	2	3	4	5	6	7
4. has general information meetings for new students regarding the sport.	1	2	3	4	5	6	7
5. talks with physical education classes regarding general or specific athletic programs.	1	2	3	4	5	6	7
6. is effective in appraising skill for identifying potential athletes who will benefit the program.	1	2	3	4	5	6	7
7. attends lower level athletic contests that potentially "feed the program."	1	2	3	4	5	6	7
8. maintains communication with lower level schools' coaches in the sport.	1	2	3	4	5	6	7
H. Rules and Regulations	1	2	3	4	5	6	7

Comments

The coach:

	1	2	3	4	5	6	7
1. knows the school and/or district policies governing athletics.	1	2	3	4	5	6	7
2. abides by these governing policies.	1	2	3	4	5	6	7
3. provides all athletes with a written statement of rules and regulations relative to their individual sport.	1	2	3	4	5	6	7
4. sends a written statement of training rules, grooming regulations and disciplinary measures to all parents.	1	2	3	4	5	6	7
5. knows the state rules regarding the sport.	1	2	3	4	5	6	7
6. knows the national rules regarding the sport.	1	2	3	4	5	6	7
7. abides by all rules and regulations.	1	2	3	4	5	6	7
8. is aware of the procedural rights of student-athletes.	1	2	3	4	5	6	7
9. makes the student-athletes aware of their procedural rights.	1	2	3	4	5	6	7
10. effectively involves team members in formulating training rules and grooming regulations.	1	2	3	4	5	6	7
11. makes certain that insurance alternatives are made known to players and parents.	1	2	3	4	5	6	7

(continued on the next page)

V.	The Coach's Knowledge of the Sport							

A. Skills and Techniques and Methods of Coaching   1 2 3 4 5 6 7

Comments

The coach:

1. is knowledgeable of the skills necessary for each position (speed, agility, ability) in the sport.   1 2 3 4 5 6 7

2. is knowledgeable of the techniques required to perform each skill (position, movement, stances) in the sport.   1 2 3 4 5 6 7

3. uses sound, up-to-date methods to teach skills and techniques (drills, scrimmage, etc.).   1 2 3 4 5 6 7

4. uses instructional media, particularly audio-visual aids such as movie film and video tape effectively.   1 2 3 4 5 6 7

5. teaches good fundamental techniques and skills.   1 2 3 4 5 6 7

B. Strategies   1 2 3 4 5 6 7

Comments

The coach:

1. is knowledgeable of up-to-date offensive strategy in the sport.   1 2 3 4 5 6 7

2. uses up-to-date offensive strategy effectively.   1 2 3 4 5 6 7

3. is knowledgeable of the theory of most offenses in the sport.   1 2 3 4 5 6 7

4. is knowledgeable of up-to-date defensive strategy in the sport.   1 2 3 4 5 6 7

5. uses up-to-date defensive strategy effectively.   1 2 3 4 5 6 7

6. is knowledgeable of the theory of most defenses in the sport.   1 2 3 4 5 6 7

7. is knowledgeable of general contest strategies.   1 2 3 4 5 6 7

8. uses general contest strategies effectively.   1 2 3 4 5 6 7

C. Scouting and Preparation for Opponent   1 2 3 4 5 6 7

Comments

The coach:

1. is knowledgeable of good scouting techniques.   1 2 3 4 5 6 7

2. has an effective scouting philosophy.   1 2 3 4 5 6 7

3. knows how to analyze films/video tape effectively.   1 2 3 4 5 6 7

4. knows how to break down and effectively use scouting reports.   1 2 3 4 5 6 7

5. scouts his/her own team and personnel.   1 2 3 4 5 6 7

D. Evaluation of Team Personnel   1 2 3 4 5 6 7

Comments

The coach:

1. effectively evaluates team personnel in the grading of films.   1 2 3 4 5 6 7

2. effectively evaluates team personnel from drill performance in practice sessions.   1 2 3 4 5 6 7

3. effectively evaluates game performance.   1 2 3 4 5 6 7

4. effectively selects personnel for positions.

85

(continued on the next page)

VI. The Coach and Public Relations

    A. Communication Skills   1   2   3   4   5   6   7
Comments
      The coach:
        1. is articulate.   1   2   3   4   5   6   7
        2. uses good grammar.   1   2   3   4   5   6   7
        3. has good writing skills.   1   2   3   4   5   6   7
    B. News Media   1   2   3   4   5   6   7
Comments
      The coach:
        1. understands the importance of good relations with   1   2   3   4   5   6   7
           the media.
        2. communicates effectively with the various news   1   2   3   4   5   6   7
           media (gets acquainted with media people, under-
           stands their problems, etc.).
        3. cooperates with the news media as well as he/she can   1   2   3   4   5   6   7
           (provides interviews, game results, statistics, etc.).
        4. encourages the news media's participation (tickets,   1   2   3   4   5   6   7
           facilities at games, invites to practice, picture day,
           etc.).
    C. Effective Interpersonal Relationships   1   2   3   4 ·5   6   7
Comments
      The coach:
        1. has good rapport with the principal.   1   2   3   4   5   6   7
        2. has good rapport with the athletic director.   1   2   3   4   5   6   7
        3. has good rapport with community agencies.   1   2   3   4   5   6   7
        4. has good rapport with parents.   1   2   3   4   5   6   7
        5. has good rapport with the faculty (school person-   1   2   3   4   5   6   7
           nel).
        6. has good rapport with the staff.   1   2   3   4   5   6   7
        7. has good rapport with officials.   1   2   3   4   5   6   7
        8. has good rapport with the student body.   1   2   3   4   5   6   7
        9. has good rapport with coaches of other sports in   1   2   3   4   5   6   7
           the program.
       10. has good rapport with professional organizations.   1   2   3   4   5   6   7

VII. The Coach's Knowledge of and Application of Kinesiological and
      Physiological Principles

    A. Movement Analysis   1   2   3   4   5   6   7
Comments
      The coach
        1. has a general knowledge of anatomical structure of   1   2   3   4   5   6   7
           the body.
        2. is knowledgeable about the mechanics of movement.   1   2   3   4   5   6   7

87

(*continued on the next page*)

3. is knowledgeable of good and safe body positions.	1	2	3	4	5	6	7
4. recognizes efficiency in movement.	1	2	3	4	5	6	7
5. can analyze movement effectively.	1	2	3	4	5	6	7
6. recognizes individual differences in movement.	1	2	3	4	5	6	7
B. Growth and Development	1	2	3	4	5	6	7

Comments

The coach:

1. is knowledgeable of physical growth and development patterns of the age group that he/she is coaching.	1	2	3	4	5	6	7
2. utilizes proper training methods for individual athletes.	1	2	3	4	5	6	7
3. is knowledgeable of proper training methods.	1	2	3	4	5	6	7
4. is knowledgeable of proper methods of strength training.	1	2	3	4	5	6	7
5. utilizes different types of training.	1	2	3	4	5	6	7
C. Nutrition	1	2	3	4	5	6	7

Comments

The coach:

1. is knowledgeable about proper nutritional diets.	1	2	3	4	5	6	7
2. knows what constitutes a proper pregame meal.	1	2	3	4	5	6	7
3. knows what constitutes proper half-time nutrition.	1	2	3	4	5	6	7
4. knows recommended safe weight-loss limits in practice and/or contests.	1	2	3	4	5	6	7

Directions for Evaluating the Assistant Coach

ASSISTANT COACH _____   SPORT _____

This evaluation instrument consists of seven major categories that are identified by Roman numerals. Within each major category there are varying numbers of subcategories that are identified by capital letters. *These are the ratings we are interested in.* To the right of each subcategory heading you will find a scale from 1–7. After you have examined the statements listed under each subcategory, circle the number for the subcategory that best represents your opinion of that area. The numerous statements (listed by Arabic numerals) are used merely as an aid to help you make a better evaluation of the subcategory rating. These statements also have the 1–7 scale; in addition, some may be answered NO or YES (if the response is NO circle 1, if the response is YES circle 7). The individual statements ratings can be "eyeballed" to determine the subcategory rating or the statements rated can be added and divided by the number of items rated (N) to determine an average subcategory rating. There may be statements that *do not apply* to your situation or *demand information* not available to you. If this is true simply *omit* responding to those items. Add any additional comments in the left-hand margin.

EXAMPLE:

III.   The Assistant Coach as a Person

A. Personal Qualities   1   2   3 ④ 5   6   7
Comments
    The assistant coach:
    1. has high moral values.   1   2   3 ④ 5   6   7
    2. sets a positive example in word, deed, and   1   2   3   4 ⑤ 6   7
       appearance.
    3. has an interest in the age group he/she is working 1   2 ③ 4   5   6   7
       with.
    4. respects students rights.   1   2 ③ 4   5   6   7

                Approximate visually or add numbers
                and divide by N for subcategory rating
                (i.e., 15 ÷ 4 = 3.75)

Assessment of the Assistant Coach

I. The Assistant Coach in the Profession							

A. Professional Preparation	1	2	3	4	5	6	7

Comments

The assistant coach:

1. is a certified teacher.	1	2	3	4	5	6	7
2. has an undergraduate degree major in physical education or a minor in coaching.	1	2	3	4	5	6	7
3. has taken a course(s) in theory of coaching in the sport.	1	2	3	4	5	6	7
4. has taken a course(s) in fundamentals of coaching in the sport.	1	2	3	4	5	6	7
5. has taken a course(s) in safety and first aid.	1	2	3	4	5	6	7
6. has taken a course(s) in care and prevention of athletic injuries.	1	2	3	4	5	6	7
7. has taken a course(s) in officiating the sport.	1	2	3	4	5	6	7
B. Educational Implications	1	2	3	4	5	6	7

Comments

The assistant coach:

1. understands the role of athletics in education.	1	2	3	4	5	6	7
2. knows the objectives of the athletic program.	1	2	3	4	5	6	7
3. is able to function well under the head coach's philosophy.	1	2	3	4	5	6	7
4. effectively performs functions as a faculty person.	1	2	3	4	5	6	7
C. Ongoing Education	1	2	3	4	5	6	7

Comments

The assistant coach:

1. has attended a clinic(s), workshop(s), seminar(s) or taken courses relating to athletic coaching in the last five years.	1	2	3	4	5	6	7
2. is an active member of any professional associations relating to athletic coaching.	1	2	3	4	5	6	7
3. subscribes to professional journals relating to athletic coaching.	1	2	3	4	5	6	7
D. Experience	1	2	3	4	5	6	7

Comments

The assistant coach:

1. participated as a player in the sport.	1	2	3	4	5	6	7
2. has had experience in coaching the sport as an undergraduate (practicum in coaching, laboratory, student teaching).	1	2	3	4	5	6	7
E. Evaluation	1	2	3	4	5	6	7

Comments

The assistant coach:

1. does an annual self-evaluation on his/her coaching ability and expertise.	1	2	3	4	5	6	7

93

(continued on the next page)

2. is evaluated by others (athletic director, principal, head coach, other assistant coaches, players) annually.   1 2 3 4 5 6 7

II. The Assistant Coach's Knowledge of and Practice of Medical Aspects of Coaching

---

A. Preparation of the Athlete for Competition   1 2 3 4 5 6 7
Comments

The assistant coach:

1. understands early season conditioning of athletes.   1 2 3 4 5 6 7
2. is knowledgeable about the factors related to exercise such as: 1 2 3 4 5 6 7
    a. fluid balance in the body (use of water in practice and games, use of salt tablets, etc.).   1 2 3 4 5 6 7
    b. environmental influences relating to body temperatures, i.e., heat, cold, humidity and altitude.   1 2 3 4 5 6 7
    c. limits imposed upon athletes with normal hearts.   1 2 3 4 5 6 7
    d. oxygen debt.   1 2 3 4 5 6 7
    e. hyperventilation.   1 2 3 4 5 6 7

B. Health and Training Techniques   1 2 3 4 5 6 7
Comments

The assistant coach:

1. is knowledgeable about good general health habits (showers, clean uniforms and undergarments in practice and contests, grooming, not drinking from the same containers, etc.).   1 2 3 4 5 6 7
2. knows the latest methods of taping.   1 2 3 4 5 6 7
3. knows how to properly use training room equipment.   1 2 3 4 5 6 7
4. uses proper measures for prevention of injuries.   1 2 3 4 5 6 7
5. knows emergency care of injuries.   1 2 3 4 5 6 7
6. is knowledgeable about proper postinjury care and rehabilitation.   1 2 3 4 5 6 7
7. is knowledgeable about how to counsel an injured athlete.   1 2 3 4 5 6 7
8. assists the head coach in formulating proper training rules that are enforceable.   1 2 3 4 5 6 7
9. is knowledgeable about training and conditioning athletes throughout a season (retain conditioning, avoid staleness, etc.).   1 2 3 4 5 6 7
10. provides for someone to properly fit equipment in order to prevent injuries.   1 2 3 4 5 6 7

95

(continued on the next page)

III. The Assistant Coach as a Person

A. Personal Qualities   1 2 3 4 5 6 7

Comments

The assistant coach:

1. has high moral values.   1 2 3 4 5 6 7
2. sets a positive example in word, deed, and appearance.   1 2 3 4 5 6 7
3. has an interest in the age group he/she is coaching.   1 2 3 4 5 6 7
4. respects student rights.   1 2 3 4 5 6 7
5. has a positive attitude and enthusiastic personality.   1 2 3 4 5 6 7
6. has emotional stability and self-control.   1 2 3 4 5 6 7
7. is flexible, adaptable in his/her attitude toward youth and societal changes.   1 2 3 4 5 6 7
8. is a good public speaker.   1 2 3 4 5 6 7
9. cooperates with school, staff, parents, and community.   1 2 3 4 5 6 7
10. keeps physically fit.   1 2 3 4 5 6 7
11. knows how to motivate athletes.   1 2 3 4 5 6 7
12. is able to disagree with or make suggestions to the head coach effectively.   1 2 3 4 5 6 7

B. Dealings with the Team   1 2 3 4 5 6 7

Comments

The assistant coach:

1. supports the head coach in his/her dealings with the team.   1 2 3 4 5 6 7
2. is fair in his/her own discipline procedures with the team.   1 2 3 4 5 6 7
3. makes certain the athletes know the training rules and other rules and requirements (such as grooming, eligibility, etc.).   1 2 3 4 5 6 7
4. makes certain the athletes know the consequences of breaking such rules and requirements.   1 2 3 4 5 6 7
5. is effective in assisting with team selection.   1 2 3 4 5 6 7
6. is honest in dealing with athletes.   1 2 3 4 5 6 7
7. is approachable to players.   1 2 3 4 5 6 7
8. uses effective guidance techniques.   1 2 3 4 5 6 7
9. respects individual differences in players.   1 2 3 4 5 6 7
10. is concerned about the athletes' academic achievements.   1 2 3 4 5 6 7

C. Loyalty to other Staff Members and the Program   1 2 3 4 5 6 7

Comments

The assistant coach:

1. is loyal to the head coach (does not criticize him/her behind his/her back).   1 2 3 4 5 6 7
2. supports the head coach's policies.   1 2 3 4 5 6 7
3. supports the head coach even on points of disagreements in policies, procedures, philosophy, etc.   1 2 3 4 5 6 7

97

(continued on the next page)

4. supports the program (not criticizing the program behind the head coach's back, etc.).   1 2 3 4 5 6 7

D. Conduct in Coaching   1 2 3 4 5 6 7

Comments

The assistant coach:

1. demonstrates good sportsmanship.   1 2 3 4 5 6 7
2. teaches good sportsmanship to players.   1 2 3 4 5 6 7
3. is respectful toward opponents.   1 2 3 4 5 6 7
4. is respectful toward officials.   1 2 3 4 5 6 7
5. is respectful and cooperative to news media personnel.   1 2 3 4 5 6 7
6. is respectful and understanding with parents.   1 2 3 4 5 6 7
7. places the importance of the athlete above winning.   1 2 3 4 5 6 7
8. would not sacrifice or compromise personal values or principles "to win."   1 2 3 4 5 6 7
9. supports other sports in the program.   1 2 3 4 5 6 7
10. supports other coaches in the program.   1 2 3 4 5 6 7

IV. General Functions and Responsibilities

A. Organization of Practice   1 2 3 4 5 6 7

Comments

The assistant coach:

1. uses the daily practice time allotted effectively.   1 2 3 4 5 6 7
2. uses facilities and equipment effectively.   1 2 3 4 5 6 7
3. is capable of assisting in planning practice sessions.   1 2 3 4 5 6 7

B. Game Management   1 2 3 4 5 6 7

Comments

The assistant coach:

1. when given a game management task to perform does his/her best in completing the task.   1 2 3 4 5 6 7

C. Purchase and Care of Equipment   1 2 3 4 5 6 7

Comments

The assistant coach:

1. follows the proper methods (policy of the school) in purchasing equipment if given that responsibility.   1 2 3 4 5 6 7
2. uses effective ways to mark and identify equipment.   1 2 3 4 5 6 7
3. keeps up-to-date equipment and inventory records.   1 2 3 4 5 6 7
4. properly cares for equipment.   1 2 3 4 5 6 7

D. Legal Aspects   1 2 3 4 5 6 7

Comments

The assistant coach:

1. knows what constitutes liability.   1 2 3 4 5 6 7
2. understands the concept of negligence.   1 2 3 4 5 6 7
3. knows the proper procedure to be taken when an injury occurs.   1 2 3 4 5 6 7

(continued on the next page)

4. knows the questionable practices that might make him/her liable (supply pills, aspirin, anticold, vitamin C, permitting players to play with an injury, etc.).　　1　2　3　4　5　6　7

5. employs reasonable and prudent conduct.　　1　2　3　4　5　6　7
6. knows how to avoid damage suits through preventive measures.　　1　2　3　4　5　6　7

E. Evaluation　　1　2　3　4　5　6　7

Comments

The assistant coach:
1. effectively assists in evaluating the progress of the program.　　1　2　3　4　5　6　7
2. is capable of assisting in evaluating the staff.　　1　2　3　4　5　6　7
3. is capable of assisting in evaluating officials effectively.　　1　2　3　4　5　6　7
4. effectively evaluates the head coach.　　1　2　3　4　5　6　7

F. Recruiting (In programs requiring this area)　　1　2　3　4　5　6　7

Comments

The assistant coach:
1. has the necessary personality to recruit effectively.　　1　2　3　4　5　6　7
2. is effective in appraising skill for identifying potential athletes who will benefit the program.　　1　2　3　4　5　6　7
3. attends lower level athletic contests that potentially "feed the program."　　1　2　3　4　5　6　7
4. maintains communication with lower level schools' coaches in the sport.　　1　2　3　4　5　6　7

G. Rules and Regulations　　1　2　3　4　5　6　7

Comments

The assistant coach:
1. knows the school and/or district policies governing athletics.　　1　2　3　4　5　6　7
2. abides by these governing policies.　　1　2　3　4　5　6　7
3. knows the state rules regarding the sport.　　1　2　3　4　5　6　7
4. knows the national rules regarding the sport.　　1　2　3　4　5　6　7
5. abides by all rules and regulations.　　1　2　3　4　5　6　7
6. is aware of the procedural rights of student-athletes.　　1　2　3　4　5　6　7
7. makes the student-athletes aware of their procedural rights.　　1　2　3　4　5　6　7

V. The Assistant Coach's Knowledge of the Sport

A. Skills, Techniques, and Methods of Coaching　　1　2　3　4　5　6　7

Comments

The assistant coach:
1. is knowledgeable of the skills necessary for each position (speed, agility, ability) in the sport.　　1　2　3　4　5　6　7

(*continued on the next page*)

2. is knowledgeable of the techniques required to perform each skill (position, movement, stances) in the sport.   1 2 3 4 5 6 7

3. uses sound up-to-date methods to teach skills and techniques (drills, scrimmage, etc.).   1 2 3 4 5 6 7

4. uses instructional media, particularly audio-visual aids such as movie film and video tape effectively.   1 2 3 4 5 6 7

5. teaches good fundamental skills and techniques.   1 2 3 4 5 6 7

B. Strategies   1 2 3 4 5 6 7

Comments

The assistant coach:

1. is knowledgeable of up-to-date offensive strategy in the sport.   1 2 3 4 5 6 7

2. uses up-to-date offensive strategy effectively.   1 2 3 4 5 6 7

3. is knowledgeable of the theory of most offenses in the sport.   1 2 3 4 5 6 7

4. is knowledgeable of up-to-date defensive strategy in the sport.   1 2 3 4 5 6 7

5. uses up-to-date defensive strategies effectively.   1 2 3 4 5 6 7

6. is knowledgeable of the theory of most defenses in the sport.   1 2 3 4 5 6 7

7. knows enough general contest strategy to assist the head coach in making effective decisions.   1 2 3 4 5 6 7

C. Scouting and Preparation for Opponent   1 2 3 4 5 6 7

Comments

The assistant coach:

1. has a good knowledge of scouting techniques.   1 2 3 4 5 6 7

2. can scout effectively.   1 2 3 4 5 6 7

3. knows how to analyze films/video tape effectively.   1 2 3 4 5 6 7

4. knows how to break down and effectively use scouting reports.   1 2 3 4 5 6 7

5. does the best job of scouting that he/she can.   1 2 3 4 5 6 7

6. accepts the task of scouting willingly.   1 2 3 4 5 6 7

D. Evaluation of Team Personnel   1 2 3 4 5 6 7

Comments

The assistant coach:

1. effectively evaluates team personnel in grading of films.   1 2 3 4 5 6 7

2. effectively evaluates team personnel from drill performance in practice sessions.   1 2 3 4 5 6 7

3. effectively evaluates game performance.   1 2 3 4 5 6 7

4. effectively assists in selecting personnel for positions.   1 2 3 4 5 6 7

(*continued on the next page*)

VI.   The Assistant Coach and Public Relations

A. Communication Skills	1	2	3	4	5	6	7

Comments

The assistant coach:

1. is articulate.	1	2	3	4	5	6	7
2. uses good grammar.	1	2	3	4	5	6	7
3. has good writing skills.	1	2	3	4	5	6	7
B. News Media	1	2	3	4	5	6	7

Comments

The assistant coach:

1. cooperates with the news media as well as he/she can. (provides interviews, game results, statistics, etc.) when cleared by the head coach.	1	2	3	4	5	6	7
2. understands the importance of good relations with the news media (value of P. R.).	1	2	3	4	5	6	7
3. understands his/her role in public relations (clears all P. R. matters to news media through the head coach, etc.).	1	2	3	4	5	6	7
C. Effective Interpersonal Relationships	1	2	3	4	5	6	7

Comments

The assistant coach:

1. has good rapport with the principal.	1	2	3	4	5	6	7
2. has good rapport with the athletic director.	1	2	3	4	5	6	7
3. has good rapport with the head coach.	1	2	3	4	5	6	7
4. has good rapport with the community agencies.	1	2	3	4	5	6	7
5. has good rapport with parents.	1	2	3	4	5	6	7
6. has good rapport with the faculty (school personnel).	1	2	3	4	5	6	7
7. has good rapport with the other staff members.	1	2	3	4	5	6	7
8. has good rapport with officials.	1	2	3	4	5	6	7
9. has good rapport with the student body.	1	2	3	4	5	6	7
10. has good rapport with coaches of other sports in the program.	1	2	3	4	5	6	7
11. has good rapport with professional organizations.	1	2	3	4	5	6	7

VII.   The Assistant Coach's Knowledge of and Application of Kinesiological and Physiological Principles

A. Movement Analysis	1	2	3	4	5	6	7

Comments

The assistant coach:	1	2	3	4	5	6	7
1. has a general knowledge of the anatomical structure of the body.	1	2	3	4	5	6	7
2. is knowledgeable about the mechanics of movement.	1	2	3	4	5	6	7
3. is knowledgeable of good and safe body positions.	1	2	3	4	5	6	7

105

(continued on the next page)

4. recognizes efficiency in movement.	1	2	3	4	5	6	7
5. can analyze movement effectively.	1	2	3	4	5	6	7
6. recognizes individual differences in movement.	1	2	3	4	5	6	7
B. Growth and Development	1	2	3	4	5	6	7

Comments

The assistant coach:

1. is knowledgeable of physical growth and development patterns of the age group that he/she is coaching.	1	2	3	4	5	6	7
2. utilizes proper training methods for individual athletes.	1	2	3	4	5	6	7
3. is knowledgeable of proper training methods.	1	2	3	4	5	6	7
4. is knowledgeable of proper methods of strength training.	1	2	3	4	5	6	7
5. utilizes different types of training.							
C. Nutrition	1	2	3	4	5	6	7

Comments

The assistant coach:

1. is knowledgeable about proper nutritional diets.	1	2	3	4	5	6	7
2. knows what constitutes a proper pregame meal.	1	2	3	4	5	6	7
3. knows what constitutes proper half-time nutrition.	1	2	3	4	5	6	7
4. knows recommended safe weight-loss limits in practice and/or contests.	1	2	3	4	5	6	7

Directions for Evaluating Officials

This evaluation instrument consists of three categories that are identified with Roman numerals. *These are the ratings we are interested in.* Within each category there are varying numbers of statements that are identified by capital letters. To the right of each category and statement you will find a scale of 1–7. After you have examined the statements listed under each category, circle the number for the category that best represents your opinion of that area. The statements are used merely as an aid to help you make a better evaluation of the three categories. Some statements may be answered NO or YES (if the response is NO circle 1, if the response is YES circle 7). The individual statements can be "eyeballed" to determine category ratings, or the statements rated can be added and divided by the number of items rated (N) to determine an average category rating. There may be statements that *do not apply* to your situation or *demand information not available* to you. If this is the case, simply *omit responding* to those items. Add any additional comments in the left-hand margin.

EXAMPLE:

III. Mechanics

Comments　　　　　　　　　　　　　　　　　　　　1　2　3　4　⑤　6　7
　The official:
　A. executes good mechanics (i.e., proper use of signals, co-　1　2　3　4　5　⑥　7
　　ordination in necessary skills, use of whistle, etc.).
　B. demonstrates knowledge of good coverage of the court,　1　2　3　4　⑤　6　7
　　field, or event.
　C. effectively lets everyone know what is going on during　1　2　3　④　5　6　7
　　the contest (i.e., players, coaches, spectators, etc.).

　　　　　　　　　　　　　Approximate visually or add numbers
　　　　　　　　　　　　　and divide by N for the category rating
　　　　　　　　　　　　　(i.e., 15 ÷ 3 = 5).

Assessment of Officials

OFFICIAL _____   DATE _____

CONTEST _____   LOCATION _____

I. Personal Qualities

Comments	1	2	3	4	5	6	7
The official:							
A. is dressed appropriately for the occasion and is well groomed.	1	2	3	4	5	6	7
B. possesses the necessary physical fitness to "stay with the contest."	1	2	3	4	5	6	7
C. demonstrates authority in a satisfactory manner.	1	2	3	4	5	6	7
D. has a thorough knowledge of the rules.	1	2	3	4	5	6	7
E. shows good judgment throughout the contest.	1	2	3	4	5	6	7
F. possesses desirable personal qualities (i.e., fairness, courage, courtesy, etc.).	1	2	3	4	5	6	7
G. is quick in making decisions when appropriate, yet has the ability to withhold judgment long enough to be sure of the decision.	1	2	3	4	5	6	7
H. renders decisions in a sharp, clear, firm, but pleasant manner.	1	2	3	4	5	6	7

II. Administration of Duties

Comments	1	2	3	4	5	6	7
The official							
A. arrives well in advance of the contest in order to give instruction to scorers, timers, captains, and supervises the warm-up period, etc.	1	2	3	4	5	6	7
B. closes the contest properly and signs appropriate score sheets or books.	1	2	3	4	5	6	7
C. conducts the contest in a manner that is safe to the contestants and spectators.	1	2	3	4	5	6	7

III. Mechanics

Comments	1	2	3	4	5	6	7
The official:							
A. executes good mechanics (i.e., proper use of signals, coordination in necessary skills, use of whistle, etc.).	1	2	3	4	5	6	7
B. demonstrates knowledge of good coverage of the court, field, or event.	1	2	3	4	5	6	7
C. effectively lets everyone know what is going on during the contest (i.e., players, coaches, spectators, etc.).	1	2	3	4	5	6	7

111

Directions for Evaluating the Athletic Trainer

TRAINER _____

This evaluation instrument consists of seven major categories that are identified by Roman numerals. Within each major category there are varying numbers of subcategories which are identified by capital letters. *These are the ratings we are interested in.* To the right of each subcategory heading you will find a scale from 1–7. After you have examined the statements listed under each subcategory, circle the number for the subcategory that best represents your opinion of that area. The numerous statements (listed by Arabic numerals) are used merely as an aid to help you make a better evaluation of the subcategory rating. These statements also have the 1–7 scale and, in addition, some may be answered NO or YES (if the response is NO circle 1, if the response is YES circle 7). The individual statements ratings can be "eyeballed" to determine the subcategory rating or the statements rated can be added and divided by the number of items rated (N) to determine an average subcategory rating. There may be statements that *do not apply* to your situation or *demand information not available* to you. If this is true simply *omit responding* to those items. Add any additional comments in the left-hand column.

EXAMPLE:

III. The Trainer as a Person	
A. Personal Qualities	1 2 3 ④ 5 6 7
Comments	
The trainer:	
1. has high moral values	1 ② 3 4 5 6 7
2. sets a positive example in word, deed, and appearance.	1 2 ③ 4 5 6 7
3. has an interest in the age group with which he/she is working	1 2 3 4 5 6 ⑦
	Approximate visually or add numbers and divide by N for the subcategory rating (i.e., $12 \div 3 = 4$).

Assessment of the Athletic Trainer

I. The Trainer in the Profession

A. Professional Preparation   1 2 3 4 5 6 7

Comments

The trainer:

1. is a certified teacher.   3 4 5 6 7
2. has an undergraduate degree major in physical education.   1 2 3 4 5 6 7
3. is a certified trainer.   1 2 3 4 5 6 7
4. has had courses in scientific basis area, physiology of exercise, kinesiology, and the prevention and care of athletic injuries.   1 2 3 4 5 6 7
5. has had courses in personal and human relations.   1 2 3 4 5 6 7
6. has had courses in coaching fundamentals.

B. Educational Implications   1 2 3 4 5 6 7

Comments

The trainer:

1. understands the role of athletics in education.   1 2 3 4 5 6 7
2. knows the objectives of the athletic program in the situation in which he/she is working.   1 2 3 4 5 6 7
3. performs his/her functions as a faculty person.   1 2 3 4 5 6 7
4. is able to function well under each head coach's philosophy.   1 2 3 4 5 6 7

C. Ongoing Education   1 2 3 4 5 6 7

Comments

The trainer:

1. attends clinics, workshops, seminars and/or courses relating to athletic training in the last two years.   1 2 3 4 5 6 7
2. is an active member of professional associations relating to athletic training.   1 2 3 4 5 6 7
3. subscribes to and reads professional journals relating to athletic training.   1 2 3 4 5 6 7

D. Experience   1 2 3 4 5 6 7

Comments

The trainer:

1. has had experience in athletic training as an undergraduate (practicum, laboratory, student assistant).   1 2 3 4 5 6 7
2. has served as assistant trainer in a high school or college.   1 2 3 4 5 6 7

E. Self-evaluation   1 2 3 4 5 6 7

Comments

The trainer:

1. completes a self-evaluation each year on his/her athletic training ability and expertise.   1 2 3 4 5 6 7

(continued on the next page)

2. asks others (doctors, athletic directors, principals,   1   2   3   4   5   6   7
students) for an evaluation of ability and expertise
each year.

II. The Trainer's Knowledge of and Practice of Athletic Training Methods

A. Preparation of the Athlete for Competition   1   2   3   4   5   6   7
Comments
    The trainer:
1. makes certain that all players have a physical exam-   1   2   3   4   5   6   7
ination report on file in the school before the player
may turn out for a sport.
2. understands factors related to exercise such as: 1   2   3   4   5   6   7
   a. fluid balance in the body (use of water in prac-   1   2   3   4   5   6   7
     tice and games, use of salt tablets, etc.).
   b. environment influences relating to body tempera-   1   2   3   4   5   6   7
     ture (heat, cold, humidity, altitude).
   c. limits imposed on athletes without heart damage.   1   2   3   4   5   6   7
   d. oxygen debt.   1   2   3   4   5   6   7
   e. hyperventilation.   1   2   3   4   5   6   7
3. keeps up-to-date medical records on each player.   1   2   3   4   5   6   7
4. works cooperatively with coaches in setting up and   1   2   3   4   5   6   7
carrying out a program of conditioning for athletes.
5. counsels and advises athletes and coaches on matters   1   2   3   4   5   6   7
pertaining to conditioning and training, such as diet,
rest, reconditioning.
6. works cooperatively with and under the direction of   1   2   3   4   5   6   7
a team doctor in respect to reconditioning programs
and postinjury care.
7. conducts in-service programs for the coaching staff   1   2   3   4   5   6   7
on the care and prevention of athletic injuries.
B. Health and Training Techniques   1   2   3   4   5   6   7
Comments
    The trainer:
1. has a good knowledge of general health habits.   1   2   3   4   5   6   7
2. knows and utilizes the latest methods of taping.   1   2   3   4   5   6   7
3. properly uses training room equipment.   1   2   3   4   5   6   7
4. uses proper measures for prevention of injuries.   1   2   3   4   5   6   7
5. can properly fit braces, guards and other devices.   1   2   3   4   5   6   7
6. knows the proper set policies and procedures for   1   2   3   4   5   6   7
emergency care of injured athletes.
7. requires written permission from a physician for an   1   2   3   4   5   6   7
injured athlete to report back for competition.
8. knows how to counsel an injured athlete.   1   2   3   4   5   6   7
9. knows how to maintain training and conditioning   1   2   3   4   5   6   7
throughout a season.

(continued on the next page)

10. knows how to properly fit standard athletic equipment.	1 2 3 4 5 6 7
11. can administer first aid to injured athletes on the field, in the gymnasium, or in the training room.	1 2 3 4 5 6 7
12. supervises the training room effectively.	

III. The Trainer as a Person

A. Personal Qualities 1 2 3 4 5 6 7
Comments

The trainer:

1. has high moral values.	1 2 3 4 5 6 7
2. sets a positive example in word, deed, and appearance.	1 2 3 4 5 6 7
3. has an interest in the age group with which he/she is working.	1 2 3 4 5 6 7
4. has a positive attitude and enthusiastic personality.	1 2 3 4 5 6 7
5. has emotional stability and self-control.	1 2 3 4 5 6 7
6. practices personal cleanliness.	1 2 3 4 5 6 7
7. maintains good physical condition.	1 2 3 4 5 6 7
8. can lead and motivate those with whom he/she works.	1 2 3 4 5 6 7
9. is able to work cooperatively with many different people.	1 2 3 4 5 6 7
10. possesses intellectual curiosity both within and outside his/her field.	1 2 3 4 5 6 7
11. has the ability to relax others with his/her wit and humor.	1 2 3 4 5 6 7
12. inspires confidence by knowing what to do, when to do it, how to do it, then doing it properly and effectively.	1 2 3 4 5 6 7
13. has a sound philosophy of life and a good philosophy of athletics.	1 2 3 4 5 6 7
14. has a sense of fair play and justice.	1 2 3 4 5 6 7
15. is the kind of person the student-athlete can look up to.	1 2 3 4 5 6 7
B. Dealings with the Team	1 2 3 4 5 6 7

Comments

The trainer:

1. serves as the liaison between the physician and the injured athlete.	1 2 3 4 5 6 7
2. serves as the liaison between the physician and head coach.	1 2 3 4 5 6 7
3. is adept in handling situations that call for a knowledge of psychological factors—knowing how to handle tense situations.	1 2 3 4 5 6 7
4. maintains a stable level of behavior and responds to irritability, obstinacy, and anger in the proper way.	1 2 3 4 5 6 7

119

(continued on the next page)

5. possesses patience and understanding in establishing and promoting effective relationships with team members.   1 2 3 4 5 6 7

6. supports the head coach in his/her dealings with the team.   1 2 3 4 5 6 7

7. treats all athletes with equality in medical procedures.   1 2 3 4 5 6 7

8. makes the athlete aware of the rules and regulations concerning the training room area.   1 2 3 4 5 6 7

9. recognizes and respects individual differences in athletes.   1 2 3 4 5 6 7

10. maintains an open positive working relationship with athletes.   1 2 3 4 5 6 7

C. Loyalty to Staff Members and the Program   1 2 3 4 5 6 7

Comments

The trainer:

1. is loyal to the coaching staff.   1 2 3 4 5 6 7
2. is loyal to the program.   1 2 3 4 5 6 7
3. supports the head coach's policies.   1 2 3 4 5 6 7

D. Conduct in Training Practices   1 2 3 4 5 6 7

Comments

The trainer:

1. demonstrates good sportsmanship.   1 2 3 4 5 6 7
2. teaches and uses proper medical techniques and practices.   1 2 3 4 5 6 7
3. is respectful and understanding of parents.   1 2 3 4 5 6 7
4. places the importance of the athlete above winning.   1 2 3 4 5 6 7
5. would not compromise his/her values or principles to win.   1 2 3 4 5 6 7
6. supports all sports and programs in the school.   1 2 3 4 5 6 7
7. does not allow pressure from coaches, parents, etc. to influence decisions on playing injured athletes.   1 2 3 4 5 6 7
8. is respectful toward officials.   1 2 3 4 5 6 7
9. is respectful toward opponents.   1 2 3 4 5 6 7
10. encourages good sportsmanship in players.   1 2 3 4 5 6 7

IV. General Functions and Responsibilities

A. Organization   1 2 3 4 5 6 7

Comments

The trainer:

1. effectively utilizes the training times allotted.   1 2 3 4 5 6 7
2. uses and maintains facilities and equipment effectively.   1 2 3 4 5 6 7

(continued on the next page)

	1	2	3	4	5	6	7
B. Game Management	1	2	3	4	5	6	7

Comments

The trainer:

	1	2	3	4	5	6	7
1. is organized and prepared for game conditions.	1	2	3	4	5	6	7
2. is prepared for team trips.	1	2	3	4	5	6	7
3. has a complete game checklist.	1	2	3	4	5	6	7
C. Purchase and Care of Equipment	1	2	3	4	5	6	7

Comments

The trainer:

	1	2	3	4	5	6	7
1. knows and follows the proper methods (policy of school) in purchasing equipment.	1	2	3	4	5	6	7
2. allows therapeutic equipment to be used only under proper supervision.	1	2	3	4	5	6	7
3. knows effective ways to mark and identify equipment.	1	2	3	4	5	6	7
4. takes proper care of training room equipment.	1	2	3	4	5	6	7
5. keeps up-to-date equipment and inventory records.	1	2	3	4	5	6	7
6. can effectively choose the most needed and right type of therapeutic equipment.	1	2	3	4	5	6	7
D. Legal Aspects	1	2	3	4	5	6	7

Comments

The trainer:

	1	2	3	4	5	6	7
1. knows what constitutes liability.	1	2	3	4	5	6	7
2. understands the concept of negligence.	1	2	3	4	5	6	7
3. knows the proper procedures to take when injuries occur.	1	2	3	4	5	6	7
4. provides proper supervision of the training room and its environs at all times.	1	2	3	4	5	6	7
5. uses only therapeutic methods he/she is qualified to use.	1	2	3	4	5	6	7
6. does not allow injured players to participate unless cleared by the team physician.	1	2	3	4	5	6	7
7. is familiar with the health and medical history of the athlete under his/her care.	1	2	3	4	5	6	7
8. understands and employs prudent and reasonable conduct.	1	2	3	4	5	6	7
9. knows how to avoid damage suits through the use of preventive measures.	1	2	3	4	5	6	7
E. Evaluation	1	2	3	4	5	6	7

Comments

The trainer:

	1	2	3	4	5	6	7
1. effectively evaluates his/her total athletic training service.	1	2	3	4	5	6	7
2. evaluates his/her staff effectively.	1	2	3	4	5	6	7
3. is capable of assisting the coaching staff in evaluating the athletic program.	1	2	3	4	5	6	7

(continued on the next page)

F. Rules and Regulations   1   2   3   4   5   6   7

Comments

The trainer:

1. abides by school and district policies regarding   1   2   3   4   5   6   7
athletics.
2. has a written policy of the rules and regulations of   1   2   3   4   5   6   7
the training room and provides each athlete with a
copy of these policies.
3. makes each parent aware of the rules and regulations   1   2   3   4   5   6   7
of the training program.

V. The Trainer's Knowledge of Sports

A. Skills, Techniques, and Methods of Coaching   1   2   3   4   5   6   7

Comments

The trainer:

1. is knowledgeable about the skills necessary for each   1   2   3   4   5   6   7
position (speed, agility, ability) in the sport.
2. effectively utilizes knowledge of skills for the pre-   1   2   3   4   5   6   7
vention of injuries (preventive taping, etc.).
3. effectively utilizes knowledge of skills for care of   1   2   3   4   5   6   7
injuries (taping, braces, diagnosis of injuries).
4. is knowledgeable about the techniques required to   1   2   3   4   5   6   7
perform each skill (positions, movements, stances).
5. effectively utilizes knowledge of techniques for pre-   1   2   3   4   5   6   7
vention of injuries (preventive taping, etc.).
6. effectively utilizes knowledge of techniques for care   1   2   3   4   5   6   7
of injuries (taping, braces, diagnosis of injury).

VI. The Trainer and Public Relations

A. Communication Skills   1   2   3   4   5   6   7

Comments

The trainer:

1. is articulate.   1   2   3   4   5   6   7
2. has good grammar.   1   2   3   4   5   6   7
3. has good writing skills.   1   2   3   4   5   6   7

B. News Media   1   2   3   4   5   6   7

Comments

The trainer:

1. cooperates with news media as well as possible   1   2   3   4   5   6   7
(provides interviews, injury results, etc. when
cleared by the head coach).
2. understands the importance of good relations with   1   2   3   4   5   6   7
the news media (value of public relations).
3. understands the trainer's role in public relations   1   2   3   4   5   6   7
(clears all P.R. matters with the head coach).

125

(continued on the next page)

	1	2	3	4	5	6	7
C. Interpersonal Relationships	1	2	3	4	5	6	7

Comments

The trainer:

	1	2	3	4	5	6	7
1. can communicate effectively with a physician.	1	2	3	4	5	6	7
2. has good rapport with the principal.	1	2	3	4	5	6	7
3. has good rapport with the athletic director.	1	2	3	4	5	6	7
4. has good rapport with the coaches.	1	2	3	4	5	6	7
5. has good rapport with the parents.	1	2	3	4	5	6	7
6. has good rapport with the faculty.	1	2	3	4	5	6	7
7. has good rapport with the staff members.	1	2	3	4	5	6	7
8. has good rapport with the officials.	1	2	3	4	5	6	7
9. has good rapport with the students.	1	2	3	4	5	6	7

VII. The Trainer's Knowledge of and Application of Kinesiological and Physiological Principles

	1	2	3	4	5	6	7
A. Movement Analysis	1	2	3	4	5	6	7

Comments

The trainer:

	1	2	3	4	5	6	7
1. has a thorough knowledge of the anatomical structure of the body.	1	2	3	4	5	6	7
2. has an in-depth knowledge about the mechanics of movement.	1	2	3	4	5	6	7
3. knows what constitutes safe body positions.	1	2	3	4	5	6	7
4. can analyze movement effectively.	1	2	3	4	5	6	7
5. knows methods of strength training.	1	2	3	4	5	6	7
6. utilizes different types of training.	1	2	3	4	5	6	7
B. Growth and Development	1	2	3	4	5	6	7

Comments

The trainer:

	1	2	3	4	5	6	7
1. knows physical growth and development patterns for the age group that he/she is training.	1	2	3	4	5	6	7
2. utilizes proper training methods for individual athletes at different age levels.	1	2	3	4	5	6	7
C. Nutrition	1	2	3	4	5	6	7

Comments

The trainer:

	1	2	3	4	5	6	7
1. knows proper nutritional habits for athletes.	1	2	3	4	5	6	7
2. knows what constitutes a proper pregame meal.	1	2	3	4	5	6	7
3. knows what constitutes proper half-time nutrition.	1	2	3	4	5	6	7
4. knows the value of using liquid and/or nutrition supplements during practice time.	1	2	3	4	5	6	7
5. knows the value of using liquids and/or nutrition supplements during game contests.	1	2	3	4	5	6	7
6. knows recommended safe weight-loss limits in practice or contests.	1	2	3	4	5	6	7
7. knows the limits within which vitamins, dextrose, etc. are to be given athletes.	1	2	3	4	5	6	7

127

PART THREE

Athletic Program Assessment Instruments

Directions for Evaluating the Athletic Program

This evaluation instrument consists of five major categories that are identified by Roman numerals. Within each major category there are varying numbers of subcategories that are identified by capital letters. *These are the ratings we are interested in.* To the right of each subcategory heading you will find a scale from 1–7. After you have examined the statements listed under each subcategory, circle the number for the subcategory that best represents your opinion of that area. The numerous statements (listed by Arabic numerals) are used merely as an aid to help you make a better evaluation of the subcategory rating. These statements also have the 1–7 scale and, in addition, some may be answered NO or YES (if the response is NO circle 1, if the response is YES circle 7). The individual statements ratings can be "eyeballed" to determine the subcategory rating or the statements rated can be added and divided by the number of items rated (N) to determine an average subcategory rating. There may be statements that *do not apply* to your situation or *demand information not available* to you. If this is true simply *omit responding* to those items. Add any additional comments in the left-hand margin.

EXAMPLE:

IV. Administration of Athletic Program	

A. Organization and Planning   1   2   ③   4   5   6   7
Comments
    1. The procedures for reaching the goals and objectives are thoroughly and clearly written.   1   2   3   4   ⑤   6   7
    2. All policies and procedures are based upon the welfare of the athletes.   ①   2   3   4   5   6   7
    3. Lines of authority are made clear to all staff.   1   2   ③   4   5   6   7

Approximate visually or add numbers and divide by N for subcategory rating (i.e., 9 ÷ 3 = 3).

Assessment of the Athletic Program

I. Relationship of the Athletic Program to the Total Educational Program

A. Purposes and Objectives of the Athletic Program   1 2 3 4 5 6 7
Comments

1. The administration of the school has a clearly written statement of goals and objectives for the athletic program.   1 2 3 4 5 6 7

2. The athletic staff, administration, faculty, student body and the community were involved in the development of the statement of the goals and objectives of the athletic program.   1 2 3 4 5 6 7

3. The statement of goals and objectives of the program is effectively made known to the athletic staff, administration, faculty, student body, and community.   1 2 3 4 5 6 7

4. All goals and objectives of the statement can be evaluated.   1 2 3 4 5 6 7

5. All athletic personnel function in accordance with the statement of goals and objectives.   1 2 3 4 5 6 7

6. The athletic program is conducted in accordance with the statement of goals and objectives.   1 2 3 4 5 6 7

7. There is sufficient flexibility and opportunity for the ongoing revision of the statement as changing conditions warrant.   1 2 3 4 5 6 7

8. Individual coaches have written statements of goals for their respective sports.   1 2 3 4 5 6 7

9. All goals are primarily concerned with the welfare of the student.   1 2 3 4 5 6 7

10. All goals and objectives are based on educational objectives.   1 2 3 4 5 6 7

11. The athletic program is an extension of the physical education department.   1 2 3 4 5 6 7

12. All new athletic personnel are made aware of the goals, policies and procedures of the athletic program.   1 2 3 4 5 6 7

13. There is no evidence that any athletic personnel operate outside the framework of the board policy.   1 2 3 4 5 6 7

14. Students have opportunities for input into the formulation and/or changes in policy-making of goals and objectives.   1 2 3 4 5 6 7

15. The athletic program supplements the physical education program.   1 2 3 4 5 6 7

16. The athletic program is subject to the same administrative control as the total educational program.   1 2 3 4 5 6 7

133

(continued on the next page)

II. Fiscal Management of the Athletic Program							

A. Revenue/Income   1 2 3 4 5 6 7
Comments

1. The policies governing the revenue and expenditure of funds for athletics are clearly stated in written form.   1 2 3 4 5 6 7
2. Policies are followed in conducting the program.   1 2 3 4 5 6 7
3. All income for athletics (school district allotments and supplemental) is a part of a general athletic fund.   1 2 3 4 5 6 7
4. Fair consideration is given to equitable distribution of funds to all sports in the program.   1 2 3 4 5 6 7
5. All coaches have a voice in determining the total budget.   1 2 3 4 5 6 7
6. All coaches have a voice in the distribution of funds to the various sports in the program.   1 2 3 4 5 6 7
7. The budget is supplemented by funds from booster clubs or special fund-raising projects.   1 2 3 4 5 6 7
8. All special fund-raising projects are approved and co-ordinated by the athletic director.   1 2 3 4 5 6 7

B. Budget   1 2 3 4 5 6 7
Comments

1. A clear, itemized, written annual athletic budget is prepared.   1 2 3 4 5 6 7
2. Students are involved in the formulation of all aspects of the budget.   1 2 3 4 5 6 7
3. The administration is kept informed on all aspects of the budget.   1 2 3 4 5 6 7
4. The athletic director is accountable for use of all funds allotted in the budget.   1 2 3 4 5 6 7
5. All coaches receive a copy of their completed budget.   1 2 3 4 5 6 7
6. Each coach is involved in the formulation of the budget for his/her sport.   1 2 3 4 5 6 7
7. Complete financial budgets and records are kept by some personnel (athletic director, bookkeeper, etc.) during the year to facilitate the proper use of the budget.   1 2 3 4 5 6 7
8. Complete financial budgets and records of past years are kept to provide information for evaluation and future planning.   1 2 3 4 5 6 7
9. There is a clearly written policy regarding accountability of coaches for their budget.   1 2 3 4 5 6 7
10. The athletic program stays within its allotted budget.   1 2 3 4 5 6 7

135

(*continued on the next page*)

11. The salaries of athletic personnel are equitable with the established salary schedules for comparable teachers.　　1　2　3　4　5　6　7

12. The athletic budget is completely supported by school district funds.　　1　2　3　4　5　6　7

13. The program operates as efficiently as it can on the allotted budget.　　1　2　3　4　5　6　7

C. Equipment　　1　2　3　4　5　6　7

Comments

1. There are clearly written policies and procedures regarding the purchase of athletic supplies and equipment.　　1　2　3　4　5　6　7

2. All coaches abide by the policies and procedures.　　1　2　3　4　5　6　7

3. Equipment and supplies in each sport are adequate and equitable to other sports in the program.　　1　2　3　4　5　6　7

4. All coaches in the program have equitable and adequate input in determining the type, amount, and quality of supplies and equipment.　　1　2　3　4　5　6　7

5. The safety and comfort of the athlete is the primary consideration in the choosing of athletic equipment.　　1　2　3　4　5　6　7

6. All coaches make periodic checks of the equipment used in their sport to insure the safety of the participants.　　1　2　3　4　5　6　7

7. Contest uniforms are attractive and players take pride in wearing them.　　1　2　3　4　5　6　7

8. Practice equipment is chosen and selected as carefully as contest equipment.　　1　2　3　4　5　6　7

9. An up-to-date inventory in all sports is kept on all equipment and supplies.　　1　2　3　4　5　6　7

10. All coaches are knowledgeable of the proper care of equipment and demand that all athletes take proper care of the equipment.　　1　2　3　4　5　6　7

11. A properly secured, properly heated, ventilated, and well-lighted facility is available for the storage of equipment for all sports.　　1　2　3　4　5　6　7

12. There is an effective set procedure for issue and return of equipment and supplies in all sports.　　1　2　3　4　5　6　7

13. A person is designated for the responsibility of the care and issue of equipment in each sport.　　1　2　3　4　5　6　7

14. All coaches assist in enforcing rules concerning the use of equipment and supplies by athletes.　　1　2　3　4　5　6　7

15. Adequate, secured individual lockers are available to all athletes in all sports.　　1　2　3　4　5　6　7

16. Coaches in all sports are required to take complete inventory of the equipment and supplies used in their sport at the end of each season.　　1　2　3　4　5　6　7

17. Clean uniforms and undergarments are issued on a regular basis in all sports.　　1　2　3　4　5　6　7

(continued on the next page)

18. All damaged equipment is kept from use until properly repaired. 1 2 3 4 5 6 7
19. Satisfactory arrangements are made for the repair and reconditioning of equipment in all sports. 1 2 3 4 5 6 7
20. Hand-me-down equipment used by B squads and JV squads is checked for condition, fitting, and comfort. 1 2 3 4 5 6 7
21. Long-range planning is effective in replacing and purchasing major equipment items. 1 2 3 4 5 6 7
22. The advantages of early buying are clearly understood by those responsible for purchasing equipment. 1 2 3 4 5 6 7
23. Both the advantages and disadvantages of bid buying are clearly understood by those responsible for purchasing equipment. 1 2 3 4 5 6 7
24. An effective method of marking equipment and supplies is used. 1 2 3 4 5 6 7
25. Adequate off-season storage facilities for equipment and supplies are provided. 1 2 3 4 5 6 7
26. The best equipment and supplies are obtained within the limits of the budget. 1 2 3 4 5 6 7

D. Officials (also see the separate assessment instrument on officials) 1 2 3 4 5 6 7
Comments

1. There are adequate dressing facilities for officials. 1 2 3 4 5 6 7
2. There is effective open communication with local, county and/or state officials' associations. 1 2 3 4 5 6 7
3. There is a clearly written policy on the procedure as to how a coach files a grievance with an official's association. 1 2 3 4 5 6 7
4. Adequate security is provided for officials during and after athletic contests. 1 2 3 4 5 6 7
5. A designated person is responsible for paying all officials at all athletic contests. 1 2 3 4 5 6 7
6. Coaches attend clinics sponsored by local, county, and state officials' associations. 1 2 3 4 5 6 7
7. Properly qualified and certified athletic officials are obtained for all contests. 1 2 3 4 5 6 7

III. Relationship of the Athletic Program to the Community

A. Public Relations 1 2 3 4 5 6 7
Comments

1. There is a cooperative effort by all coaches in the program to promote good relations with the total community (news media, parents, students, etc.). 1 2 3 4 5 6 7

139

(continued on the next page)

2. Dates and times of all athletic contests are publicized in the media.　　1　2　3　4　5　6　7

3. The community is informed and allowed an input before any major changes are made in the athletic program.　　1　2　3　4　5　6　7

4. A designated person is responsible for reporting the results of each athletic contest to the school and/ or local newspapers.　　1　2　3　4　5　6　7

5. Season tickets are sent to all pertinent news media people.　　1　2　3　4　5　6　7

6. Adequate accommodations in press box, scoring-table, or similar facility are available for news media people.　　1　2　3　4　5　6　7

7. The community is informed in writing of the school athletic program objectives and policies.　　1　2　3　4　5　6　7

8. All coaches understand the importance and principles of good public relations.　　1　2　3　4　5　6　7

B. Community　　1　2　3　4　5　6　7
Comments

1. Members of the community are made aware of the goals and objectives of the program.　　1　2　3　4　5　6　7

2. All coaches attempt to visit the parents of all athletes involved in their program.　　1　2　3　4　5　6　7

3. Coaches send letters to all parents of their players that outline the goals and objectives of the school athletic program.　　1　2　3　4　5　6　7

4. The athletic program is meeting the needs and interests of the community.　　1　2　3　4　5　6　7

5. The community supports all areas of the athletic program.　　1　2　3　4　5　6　7

6. There is coordination and cooperation between the athletic program and the community in regards to scheduling of practice times and contest times so as not to conflict with community activities.　　1　2　3　4　5　6　7

7. Parents and community groups are given advance notice of all athletic events as far ahead of time as possible.　　1　2　3　4　5　6　7

8. All school athletic facilities are made available to the community whenever they are not in use for school activities.　　1　2　3　4　5　6　7

C. Recruitment of Players　　1　2　3　4　5　6　7
Comments

1. Coaches have an effective systematic means of recruiting athletes from the lower level schools.　　1　2　3　4　5　6　7

2. There are general informational meetings for new students regarding the athletic program.　　1　2　3　4　5　6　7

141

(*continued on the next page*)

3. Material regarding the athletic program is sent to all parents and students at the beginning of each school year.   1   2   3   4   5   6   7

4. Coaches talk with physical education classes regarding general or individual athletic programs.   1   2   3   4   5   6   7

5. Coaches effectively review physical education aptitude tests in an attempt to identify highly skilled athletes.   1   2   3   4   5   6   7

6. Coaches regularly attend lower level school athletic contests.   1   2   3   4   5   6   7

7. Coaches maintain effective communication with lower level school coaches in their respective sports.   1   2   3   4   5   6   7

8. All coaches abide by all league and national rules and regulations in recruiting.   1   2   3   4   5   6   7

9. An attempt is made to assign coaches to recruiting areas according to their familiarity with the areas.   1   2   3   4   5   6   7

10. Geographical areas with an abundance of gifted athletes are thoroughly covered in the recruiting program.   1   2   3   4   5   6   7

11. An attempt is made to recruit local talent first and with the most vigor.   1   2   3   4   5   6   7

12. An attempt is made to recruit multisport athletes.   1   2   3   4   5   6   7

13. All potential recruiters are utilized and well trained (i.e., alumni, community leaders, students, faculty, principals, counselors).   1   2   3   4   5   6   7

14. The admissions office is used effectively In recruiting by keeping them informed of prospects, sending materials to prospects, etc.   1   2   3   4   5   6   7

15. Lower level school coaches are cultivated (i.e., visitations, speaking at their banquets, offering clinics, and friendship).   1   2   3   4   5   6   7

16. Effective methods are used in evaluating the physical, mental, and character attributes of student-athletes.   1   2   3   4   5   6   7

17. A thorough and effective procedure is used in recruiting athletes (letters to the coach, letters to guidance counselor for grades and test scores, information card to coach, contact with the prospective athlete, etc.).   1   2   3   4   5   6   7

18. There is no evidence of unethical recruiting.   1   2   3   4   5   6   7

19. Coaches cooperate with recruiters and help the student-athlete to effectively choose a higher level school to attend.   1   2   3   4   5   6   7

143

(*continued on the next page*)

IV. Administration of Athletic Program							

A. Organization and Planning   1   2   3   4   5   6   7

Comments

1. The procedures for reaching the goals and objectives of the athletic program are thoroughly and clearly written.   1   2   3   4   5   6   7

2. All policies and procedures are based upon the welfare of the athlete.   1   2   3   4   5   6   7

3. Lines of authority are made clear to all staff.   1   2   3   4   5   6   7

4. Grievance procedures are clearly written out and made known to all staff.   1   2   3   4   5   6   7

5. Provisions are made for all invested people to have input into the decision-making process (students, faculty, staff, and community).   1   2   3   4   5   6   7

6. The athletic department has regularly scheduled meetings to develop policy and resolve problems.   1   2   3   4   5   6   7

7. There are clearly written policies concerning selection, job description, and retention of athletic personnel.   1   2   3   4   5   6   7

8. Suggestions concerning changes in future planning can be easily made to the school administration.   1   2   3   4   5   6   7

9. There is a defined, written process to evaluate the effectiveness of the policies.   1   2   3   4   5   6   7

B. Scheduling   1   2   3   4   5   6   7

Comments

1. All scheduling of athletic contests is done on the basis of what is good for the students.   1   2   3   4   5   6   7

2. The scheduling of athletic contests is done on an equitable basis for all sports.   1   2   3   4   5   6   7

3. The scheduling of athletic contests is effective in regard to the balance ratio of home/away contests.   1   2   3   4   5   6   7

4. The scheduling of facilities is done on an equitable basis for all sports.   1   2   3   4   5   6   7

5. The scheduling of contests is done with the total community in mind so that conflicts with community programs are avoided.   1   2   3   4   5   6   7

6. Scheduling is done so that athletes will miss a minimum of classroom time.   1   2   3   4   5   6   7

7. Scheduling is done so that as many games as possible can be played on the same date and trip (boys' varsity contests, girls' varsity contests, B games, frosh games, etc.).   1   2   3   4   5   6   7

8. All game arrangements (i.e., time, date, place, etc.) are taken care of with adequate advance notice.   1   2   3   4   5   6   7

9. Scheduling is developed on the basis of equitable competition in all sports.   1   2   3   4   5   6   7

145

(*continued on the next page*)

10. All coaches participate in the scheduling of contests in their sports.   1 2 3 4 5 6 7

11. Efforts are made to keep the overlapping of seasonal scheduling at a minimum.   1 2 3 4 5 6 7

12. Competitive schedules of all sports are well advertised.   1 2 3 4 5 6 7

13. The number of contests scheduled in any sport is consistent with state association or national rules and regulations.   1 2 3 4 5 6 7

14. The number of scheduled contests is within the financial capabilities of the school.   1 2 3 4 5 6 7

15. The scheduling of facilities is coordinated with physical education.   1 2 3 4 5 6 7

C. Transportation   1 2 3 4 5 6 7

Comments

1. There is a clearly written policy regarding how to request transportation.   1 2 3 4 5 6 7

2. There are clearly written policies regarding what type of transportation may be used to and from athletic contests (i.e., public carrier, school bus, private car).   1 2 3 4 5 6 7

3. A person is designated the responsibility for double checking all transportation requests.   1 2 3 4 5 6 7

4. There are clearly written rules and regulations regarding student conduct on athletic trips.   1 2 3 4 5 6 7

5. The legal implications concerning the transportation of athletes and other personnel are understood.   1 2 3 4 5 6 7

6. Equitable transportation is provided for all sports.   1 2 3 4 5 6 7

D. Personnel   1 2 3 4 5 6 7

Comments

1. All coaching personnel meet standards of state and local certification requirements.   1 2 3 4 5 6 7

2. All coaches are duly qualified to coach their sport.   1 2 3 4 5 6 7

3. Coaches are selected who have values that are in accordance with community standards of morality.   1 2 3 4 5 6 7

4. Whenever a sport is so popular that it needs more levels of teams, additional contests are scheduled for these levels.   1 2 3 4 5 6 7

5. There are adequate staff hired for all sports.   1 2 3 4 5 6 7

6. Nonteaching personnel utilized in the program comply with the state regulations for such people.   1 2 3 4 5 6 7

7. Nonteaching personnel are utilized effectively in the program.   1 2 3 4 5 6 7

8. All faculty privileges and benefits (i.e., tenure, etc.) are available to athletic personnel.   1 2 3 4 5 6 7

9. All athletic personnel are supportive of other staff members and their programs.   1 2 3 4 5 6 7

(continued on the next page)

10. All athletic personnel effectively perform their functions as faculty members (i.e., teaching, committees, etc.).   1 2 3 4 5 6 7

11. Athletic personnel carry the equivalent workload (i.e., teaching, administration, etc.) as all other faculty.   1 2 3 4 5 6 7

12. Athletic personnel are active members in the professional organizations related to their teaching and coaching areas.   1 2 3 4 5 6 7

13. All athletic personnel have positive influence on athletes.   1 2 3 4 5 6 7

14. All coaches show respect for the letter and intent of all rules and regulations.   1 2 3 4 5 6 7

15. All coaches have respect for authority, understand and follow lines of authority. (Don't try to go over someone's head.)   1 2 3 4 5 6 7

16. All coaches exhibit and actively teach good sportsmanship.   1 2 3 4 5 6 7

17. All coaches show maturity and reasonable self-control in contests and with athletes, officials, faculty, parents, news media, staff, administration, and other coaches.   1 2 3 4 5 6 7

18. All coaches have a high respect for the human dignity of athletes, parents, and opposing coaches.   1 2 3 4 5 6 7

19. All coaches show professionalism through attendance at in-service programs and clinics.   1 2 3 4 5 6 7

20. The salaries for coaches are equitable in all sports.   1 2 3 4 5 6 7

21. All coaches are coaching because of their commitment to—and qualifications for—coaching and not just for a salary supplement.   1 2 3 4 5 6 7

22. All athletic personnel emphasize the importance of academics.   1 2 3 4 5 6 7

23. Harmonious relations, mutual respect, and cooperation exist among members of the athletic staff.   1 2 3 4 5 6 7

E. Contest Management   1 2 3 4 5 6 7

Comments

1. There is a thorough written checklist for game management for all sports.   1 2 3 4 5 6 7

2. The game management checklist covers all pregame, game, and postgame responsibilities thoroughly and effectively.   1 2 3 4 5 6 7

3. All contests start on time.   1 2 3 4 5 6 7

4. Visiting teams are contacted well in advance and informed in writing about game plans and procedures.

5. Arrangements are made for supervisory personnel to be present at all sport contests.   1 2 3 4 5 6 7

6. All half-time entertainment is well planned in advance.   1 2 3 4 5 6 7

149

(continued on the next page)

7. Facilities and any special equipment used by the home team (phones, walkie-talkies, blackboards) are available to the visiting team. 1 2 3 4 5 6 7

8. Officials are contacted and given all pertinent information about the site, time, date, and other details well in advance. 1 2 3 4 5 6 7

9. Possible problem areas are anticipated and prepared for effectively (extra ticket booths, police, parking, etc.). 1 2 3 4 5 6 7

10. The visiting team is treated as a "guest" and given all due consideration by the home team. 1 2 3 4 5 6 7

F. Relations with League and State Associations 1 2 3 4 5 6 7
Comments

1. The school is an active participating member in the state association. 1 2 3 4 5 6 7

2. All coaches of all sports are provided with a state association handbook. 1 2 3 4 5 6 7

3. All athletic personnel know and adhere to the state and national association rules. 1 2 3 4 5 6 7

4. All coaches are provided with a copy of all league rules and regulations. 1 2 3 4 5 6 7

5. All athletic personnel know and adhere to league rules. 1 2 3 4 5 6 7

6. All athletes are made aware of the rules and regulations of the state association and league as they pertain to them. 1 2 3 4 5 6 7

7. All coaches adhere to state regulations concerning sports seasons. 1 2 3 4 5 6 7

8. All sports in the program adhere to state and/or league regulations concerning number of contests allowed. 1 2 3 4 5 6 7

9. All sports in the program adhere to state/league/school policies concerning awards. 1 2 3 4 5 6 7

10. Awards given in all sports are equitable to each other. 1 2 3 4 5 6 7

11. Established sport seasons permit the maximum conditioning and development of participants. 1 2 3 4 5 6 7

G. Evaluation
Comments

1. All sport programs are effectively and unbiasedly evaluated yearly by the administration. 1 2 3 4 5 6 7

2. All coaches are effectively and unbiasedly evaluated yearly in writing by the administration. 1 2 3 4 5 6 7

3. A written evaluation of assistant coaches is conducted annually by the head coach in each sport. 1 2 3 4 5 6 7

4. All coaches have the opportunity to evaluate the total program and the administration of the program yearly in written form. 1 2 3 4 5 6 7

(*continued on the next page*)

5. There is an effective method for students, athletes, and nonathletes, to evaluate the program yearly.   1 2 3 4 5 6 7

6. There is an effective method for members of the community to evaluate the program yearly.   1 2 3 4 5 6 7

7. There is an effective method for evaluating whether the goals and objectives of the program are being met.   1 2 3 4 5 6 7

8. There is an effective method for evaluating yearly all personnel involved in the program.   1 2 3 4 5 6 7

9. There is an effective method for evaluating each sport in the program yearly.   1 2 3 4 5 6 7

10. The program is considered valuable by the student body.   1 2 3 4 5 6 7

V. Student in the Athletic Program

A. Participation (i.e., meeting needs of students)   1 2 3 4 5 6 7

Comments

1. The welfare of the student-athlete is placed above all other considerations in the program.   1 2 3 4 5 6 7

2. Students are given an opportunity to decide which sports should be offered in the program.   1 2 3 4 5 6 7

3. The program offers a wide variety of sports that permit all interested students to participate.   1 2 3 4 5 6 7

4. All interested students have equitable opportunity to participate in some phase of the program.   1 2 3 4 5 6 7

5. If unable to make a varsity team, there are enough levels of competition for all interested students to be able to compete.   1 2 3 4 5 6 7

6. The objectives of the athletic program are made known to all students.   1 2 3 4 5 6 7

7. Students are encouraged to participate in a variety of sports.   1 2 3 4 5 6 7

8. Students are allowed to participate in only one sport at a time.   1 2 3 4 5 6 7

9. All students are required to have a complete physical examination before turning out for a sport.   1 2 3 4 5 6 7

10. Students have the opportunity to participate in the formulation of objectives, policies, rules, and regulations of athletics in the school.   1 2 3 4 5 6 7

11. Athletic personnel are aware of the procedural rights of students.   1 2 3 4 5 6 7

12. Students are made aware of procedures in appealing an arbitrary decision on the part of a coach or administrator.   1 2 3 4 5 6 7

13. The student body is made to feel a part of the program.   1 2 3 4 5 6 7

153

(continued on the next page)

14. The student body is considered first in opportunities to attend contests.   1 2 3 4 5 6 7

15. Insurance programs and options are made known to athletes.   1 2 3 4 5 6 7

16. All students are required to have written permission from parents/guardians before they may turn out for any sport.   1 2 3 4 5 6 7

17. Opportunities are available for individuals who excel in a sport where there is not a fully developed program to compete and to develop his/her potential (ice skating, gymnastics, swimming, etc.).   1 2 3 4 5 6 7

B. School Spirit   1 2 3 4 5 6 7

Comments

1. The objectives and values of the athletic program are communicated effectively to the faculty and student body.   1 2 3 4 5 6 7

2. Students who are not on athletic teams are made to feel part of the athletic program.   1 2 3 4 5 6 7

3. Students who do not have the ability to compete in the athletic program are encouraged to be involved in intramural sports.   1 2 3 4 5 6 7

4. Athletics are having a positive effect on the student body.   1 2 3 4 5 6 7

5. The student body feels that the athletic teams are their teams (i.e., they represent the school, the student individually, etc.).   1 2 3 4 5 6 7

6. All athletic personnel assume roles of leadership and/or involvement in active support of other school programs (debate, etc.).   1 2 3 4 5 6 7

7. All athletic personnel have empathy for and work effectively with students who are nonathletes.   1 2 3 4 5 6 7

8. All athletic personnel respect and support other departments' programs.   1 2 3 4 5 6 7

9. All athletes are held to the same level of scholastic performance as other students.   1 2 3 4 5 6 7

10. All athletes are required to attend school and classes on the days of contests.   1 2 3 4 5 6 7

11. The program serves as a rallying point, focus for loyalty and pride for the community.   1 2 3 4 5 6 7

12. The program serves as a rallying point, focus for loyalty and pride for the student body.   1 2 3 4 5 6 7

C. Awards   1 2 3 4 5 6 7

Comments

1. Some type of awards presentation is arranged at the end of each season for all athletes in each sport.   1 2 3 4 5 6 7

2. Parents and community members are invited to the awards presentation.   1 2 3 4 5 6 7

155

(*continued on the next page*)

3. Nonparticipating students are invited to the awards presentation.   1   2   3   4   5   6   7

4. Only the awards that are authorized by national or state associations, league rules, or school policy are given to athletes.   1   2   3   4   5   6   7

5. Coaches, in cooperation with the administration, plan the award system.   1   2   3   4   5   6   7

6. Outside groups (booster clubs, etc.) are discouraged from giving awards to athletes except through proper channels.   1   2   3   4   5   6   7

7. Outside groups are informed about all policies and rules and regulations regarding awards given to athletes.   1   2   3   4   5   6   7

8. All athletic awards are the same for each sport in the program.   1   2   3   4   5   6   7

D. Health Considerations   1   2   3   4   5   6   7

Comments

1. Arrangements are made to have a physician attend all athletic contests when appropriate.   1   2   3   4   5   6   7

2. Arrangements are made to have medical service available at all practices and game situations.   1   2   3   4   5   6   7

3. All coaches are required to have a first aid certificate.   1   2   3   4   5   6   7

4. Students are required to have a health insurance policy before being allowed to participate.   1   2   3   4   5   6   7

5. Athletes are required to take a physical examination before trying out for an athletic team.   1   2   3   4   5   6   7

6. All facilities are checked periodically to make certain they meet fire and safety code requirements.   1   2   3   4   5   6   7

7. Lighting in all sport facilities meets at least minimum standards.   1   2   3   4   5   6   7

8. Playing areas are periodically checked to provide maximum safety.   1   2   3   4   5   6   7

9. There is an adequately set, written district procedure for athletic personnel to follow in case of serious injury to an athlete.   1   2   3   4   5   6   7

10. There is sufficient practice time for the coaches to properly train the athletes before participation in contests.   1   2   3   4   5   6   7

11. Daily laundry of practice apparel (socks, T-shirts, etc.) is provided by the school.   1   2   3   4   5   6   7

12. If the school does not provide for daily laundry of practice apparel, there is a policy that aids students in keeping practice apparel clean.   1   2   3   4   5   6   7

13. Cleaning/laundry service is provided by the school for contest apparel (uniforms, etc.).   1   2   3   4   5   6   7

14. If cleaning/laundry service is not provided by the school for contest apparel, there is a policy that aids students in keeping contest apparel clean.   1   2   3   4   5   6   7

157

(continued on the next page)

E. Student Aid   1 2 3 4 5 6 7

Comments

  1. Provisions and/or alternatives are provided for those athletes who cannot afford athletic fees (i.e., laundry fees, physical exams, etc.).   1 2 3 4 5 6 7

  2. Provisions and/or alternatives are provided for those students who cannot afford athletic equipment normally provided by the athlete (shoes, socks, etc.).   1 2 3 4 5 6 7

  3. The administration and coaching staff make certain that athletes are not given special privileges not available to the entire student body.   1 2 3 4 5 6 7

F. Relations with League and State Associations   1 2 3 4 5 6 7

Comments

  1. All athletes are made aware of the rules and regulations of the state association and league as they pertain to them.   1 2 3 4 5 6 7

159

Directions for Evaluating a Specific Sport

SPORT _____

   This evaluation instrument consists of five major categories that are identified by Roman numerals. Within each major category there are varying numbers of subcategories that are identified by capital letters. *These are the ratings we are interested in.* To the right of each subcategory heading you will find a scale from 1–7. After you have examined the statements listed under each subcategory, circle the number for the subcategory that best represents your opinion of that area. The numerous statements (listed by Arabic numerals) are used merely as an aid to help you make a better evaluation of the subcategory rating. These statements also have the 1–7 scale and, in addition, some may be answered NO or YES (if the response is NO circle 1, if the response is YES circle 7). The individual statements ratings can be "eyeballed" to determine the subcategory rating or the statements rated can be added and divided by the number of items rated (N) to determine an average subcategory rating. There may be statements that *do not apply* to your situation or *demand information not available* to you. If this is true, simply *omit responding* to those items. Add any additional comments in the left-hand margin.

   EXAMPLE:

V. Student in the Sport Program

   A. Participation   1   2   3   4   5   ⑥   7
   Comments
     1. The welfare of the student-athlete is placed above all 1   2   3   4   ⑤   6   7
        other considerations in the program.
     2. The program offers enough levels of competition to 1   2   3   4   5   ⑥   7
        permit all interested students to participate.
     3. All interested students have equitable opportunity 1   2   3   4   5   6   ⑦
        to try out and participate.

                                  Approximate visually or add numbers
                                  and divide by N for subcategory rating
                                  (i.e., $18 \div 3 = 6$).

Assessment of a Sport Program

I. Relationship to the Total Educational Program

A. Goals and Objectives   1 2 3 4 5 6 7
Comments

1. There is a clearly written statement of goals and objectives for the sport.   1 2 3 4 5 6 7
2. The goals and objectives are primarily concerned with the welfare of the student.   1 2 3 4 5 6 7
3. All goals and objectives are educationally sound.   1 2 3 4 5 6 7
4. The coach understands the place of and implications of the sport program in relation to the total educational program.   1 2 3 4 5 6 7
5. Goals related to the development of character are being realized (spiritual, moral, values, etc.).   1 2 3 4 5 6 7
6. Goals related to the development of cooperation and competition are being realized (sportsmanship, leadership, social, etc.).   1 2 3 4 5 6 7
7. Goals related to physical values are being realized (biological, skill development, etc.).   1 2 3 4 5 6 7
8. Goals related to emotional and psychological development are being realized (self-control, mental preparation, mental toughness, etc.).   1 2 3 4 5 6 7
9. The win-loss record is satisfactory.   1 2 3 4 5 6 7
10. Students have opportunity for input into the formulation and/or changes of the policy-making of goals and objectives.

II. Fiscal Management

A. Revenue/Income   1 2 3 4 5 6 7
Comments

1. There is a clear written policy controlling the revenue and expenditure of funds.   1 2 3 4 5 6 7
2. The policies are known, understood, and followed in conducting the sport.   1 2 3 4 5 6 7
3. The sport receives an equitable share of the total athletic funds.   1 2 3 4 5 6 7
4. The sport receives an equitable share of money raised by special projects and/or booster clubs.   1 2 3 4 5 6 7
5. Special fund raising projects are approved and coordinated by the athletic director.   1 2 3 4 5 6 7

163

(continued on the next page)

B. Budget	1	2	3	4	5	6	7

Comments

1. There is an annual itemized written budget prepared. — 1 2 3 4 5 6 7
2. The head coach receives a copy of the finalized sport budget. — 1 2 3 4 5 6 7
3. The administration is kept informed about all aspects of the budget. — 1 2 3 4 5 6 7
4. The sport stays within its allotted budget. — 1 2 3 4 5 6 7
5. Complete financial budgets and records of past years are kept to provide information for evaluation and planning. — 1 2 3 4 5 6 7
6. The coach is accountable for use of all funds allotted to the sport (funds from the budget and supplemental funds). — 1 2 3 4 5 6 7
7. The sport operates as efficiently as it can on the allotted budget. — 1 2 3 4 5 6 7
8. Supplemental funds are used properly. — 1 2 3 4 5 6 7
9. Supplemental salaries and/or release time for personnel involved are equitable to supplemental salaries/release time of personnel involved in other sports in the athletic program. — 1 2 3 4 5 6 7
10. The salaries of personnel involved are equitable with the established salary schedule for comparable teachers. — 1 2 3 4 5 6 7

C. Equipment	1	2	3	4	5	6	7

Comments

1. Equipment is effectively marked and identified. — 1 2 3 4 5 6 7
2. An up-to-date inventory is kept on all equipment and supplies. — 1 2 3 4 5 6 7
3. The equipment is cared for properly. — 1 2 3 4 5 6 7
4. Adequate equipment and supplies are provided for all participants at all levels in the sport. — 1 2 3 4 5 6 7
5. Long-range planning is done to provide for replacement and purchase of major equipment items. — 1 2 3 4 5 6 7
6. Properly secured, properly heated, ventilated, and well-lighted facilities are provided for storage of equipment. — 1 2 3 4 5 6 7
7. Adequate arrangements are made for the repair and reconditioning of equipment. — 1 2 3 4 5 6 7
8. Program policies regarding purchase of athletic supplies and equipment are followed. — 1 2 3 4 5 6 7
9. The safety and comfort of the athlete is given primary consideration in choosing athletic equipment. — 1 2 3 4 5 6 7
10. Periodic checks of the equipment are made to insure the safety of the participants. — 1 2 3 4 5 6 7
11. Contest uniforms are attractive so that players take pride in wearing them. — 1 2 3 4 5 6 7

(*continued on the next page*)

12. Practice equipment is chosen and selected as carefully as contest equipment.	1	2	3	4	5	6	7
13. An effective set procedure for issue and return of equipment and supplies is utilized.	1	2	3	4	5	6	7
14. A designated person is responsible for the care and issue of equipment.	1	2	3	4	5	6	7
15. All coaches assist in enforcing rules/policies concerning the use of equipment and supplies.	1	2	3	4	5	6	7
16. Adequate secured individual lockers are available to the athletes in the sport.	1	2	3	4	5	6	7
17. A complete inventory of equipment and supplies used in the sport is taken at the end of each season.	1	2	3	4	5	6	7
18. Clean uniforms and undergarments are issued on a regular basis.	1	2	3	4	5	6	7
19. Damaged equipment is kept from use until properly repaired.	1	2	3	4	5	6	7
20. Long-range planning is effective in purchasing and replacing major equipment items.	1	2	3	4	5	6	7
21. Adequate off-season storage facilities for equipment is provided.	1	2	3	4	5	6	7
22. The best equipment and supplies are obtained within the limits of the budget.	1	2	3	4	5	6	7

D. Officials (also see the separate assessment instrument on officials)
Comments

1. Adequate dressing facilities are provided for officials.	1	2	3	4	5	6	7
2. There is effective, open communication with local, county, and/or state officials' association.	1	2	3	4	5	6	7
3. There is a clear, written policy on the procedure about how a grievance may be filed with an officials' association.	1	2	3	4	5	6	7
4. Adequate security is provided for officials during and after contests.	1	2	3	4	5	6	7
5. A designated person is responsible for paying officials at contests.	1	2	3	4	5	6	7
6. Coaches in the sport attend clinics sponsored by local, county, and state officials' associations.	1	2	3	4	5	6	7
7. Properly qualified and certified officials are obtained for all contests.	1	2	3	4	5	6	7

III. Relationship to the Community

A. Public Relations	1	2	3	4	5	6	7

Comments

1. The community is informed and allowed input before any major changes are made in the sport program.	1	2	3	4	5	6	7

167

(continued on the next page)

2. The dates and times of all contests are publicized in the media.   1 2 3 4 5 6 7

3. An attempt is made to introduce the sport team and participants to the general public at the beginning of each season.   1 2 3 4 5 6 7

4. A designated person is responsible for reporting the results of each sports contest to the school and/or local newspaper.   1 2 3 4 5 6 7

5. Season tickets are sent to all pertinent news media people.   1 2 3 4 5 6 7

6. Adequate accommodations in the press box, scoring table, or any similar facility are made available for news media people.   1 2 3 4 5 6 7

7. Coaches in the sport make an effort to promote good relations with the total community (parents, faculty, students, etc.).   1 2 3 4 5 6 7

8. Coaches understand the importance and principles of good public relations.   1 2 3 4 5 6 7

B. Community   1 2 3 4 5 6 7

Comments

1. The community supports the program.   1 2 3 4 5 6 7

2. The program is meeting the needs of the community.

3. Community facilities are made available for the sport if needed.   1 2 3 4 5 6 7

4. Facilities used in the sport are made available to the community whenever they are not in use for school needs.   1 2 3 4 5 6 7

5. Parents are informed in writing about all policies in the sport (trip arrangements, insurance programs, codes of conduct, etc.).   1 2 3 4 5 6 7

6. The community at large is made aware of the goals and objectives of the sport.   1 2 3 4 5 6 7

7. Letters are sent to parents of players outlining the goals and objectives of the program.   1 2 3 4 5 6 7

8. Parents and community groups are given advanced notice of all events as far ahead of time as possible.   1 2 3 4 5 6 7

9. The coach attempts to visit the parents of all athletes involved in the sport.   1 2 3 4 5 6 7

C. Recruitment of players   1 2 3 4 5 6 7

Comments

1. An effective systematic means of recruiting athletes from lower level schools has been established.   1 2 3 4 5 6 7

2. General information meetings regarding the program are held for new students.   1 2 3 4 5 6 7

3. Material regarding the program is sent to all parents and students at an appropriate time of the school year.   1 2 3 4 5 6 7

169

(continued on the next page)

4. Coaches talk periodically with physical education classes regarding the program.   1 2 3 4 5 6 7

5. Coaches effectively review physical education aptitude tests in an attempt to identify highly skilled athletes.   1 2 3 4 5 6 7

6. Coaches regularly attend lower level school athletic contests.   1 2 3 4 5 6 7

7. Coaches maintain effective communication with lower level school coaches.   1 2 3 4 5 6 7

8. All coaches abide by all league and national rules and regulations in recruiting practices.   1 2 3 4 5 6 7

9. An attempt is made to assign coaches to recruiting areas that they are familiar with.   1 2 3 4 5 6 7

10. Areas with an abundance of gifted athletes are thoroughly covered in the recruiting program.   1 2 3 4 5 6 7

11. An attempt is made to recruit local talent first and with the most vigor.   1 2 3 4 5 6 7

12. An attempt is made to recruit multisport athletes.   1 2 3 4 5 6 7

13. All potential recruiters are utilized and well trained (alumni, community leaders, students, faculty, principals, counselors, etc.).   1 2 3 4 5 6 7   1 2 3 4 5 6 7

14. The admissions office is used effectively in recruiting by keeping them informed of prospects, sending material to prospects, etc.   1 2 3 4 5 6 7

15. Lower level school coaches are cultivated effectively (visitations, speaking at banquets, offering clinics, etc.).   1 2 3 4 5 6 7

16. Effective methods are used in evaluating physical, mental, and character attributes of potential student athletes.   1 2 3 4 5 6 7

17. A thorough and effective procedure is used in recruiting athletes (letters to coaches, letters to counselors for grades and test scores, information cards to coaches, contact with the prospective athlete, etc.).   1 2 3 4 5 6 7

18. All recruiters' ethics are completely above reproach.   1 2 3 4 5 6 7

19. Coaches cooperate with recruiters and help student-athletes to effectively choose a higher level school to attend.   1 2 3 4 5 6 7

IV. Administration of the Program

A. Organization and Planning   1 2 3 4 5 6 7

Comments

1. The goals and objectives of the program as adopted by the school administration are thoroughly and clearly written.   1 2 3 4 5 6 7

171

(*continued on the next page*)

2. The procedures for reaching the goals and objectives of the program are thoroughly and clearly written.   1 2 3 4 5 6 7

3. Grievance procedures are clearly written out and made known to all staff members.   1 2 3 4 5 6 7

4. Provisions are made for all invested people to have input into the decision-making process of goals and objectives for the program (students, faculty, staff, and community).   1 2 3 4 5 6 7

5. Coaches are involved in regularly scheduled meetings to develop policy and resolve problems.   1 2 3 4 5 6 7

6. There are clearly written policies concerning selection, job description, and retention of personnel in the program.   1 2 3 4 5 6 7

7. Suggestions concerning changes in future planning can be easily made to the school administration.   1 2 3 4 5 6 7

8. Practice sessions are efficiently organized.   1 2 3 4 5 6 7

9. All aspects of the program are properly evaluated.   1 2 3 4 5 6 7

10. The head coach turns in a yearly written evaluation of each person on his staff to the athletic director.   1 2 3 4 5 6 7

B. Scheduling   1 2 3 4 5 6 7

Comments

1. All scheduling of contests is done on the basis of what is good for the students.   1 2 3 4 5 6 7

2. Scheduling of contests is done on an equitable basis with other sports.   1 2 3 4 5 6 7

3. Scheduling of contests is effective in regard to the balance ratio of home/away contests.   1 2 3 4 5 6 7

4. Scheduling of facilities is done on an equitable basis with other sports.   1 2 3 4 5 6 7

5. Scheduling of contests is done with the total community in mind so that conflicts with community programs are avoided.   1 2 3 4 5 6 7

6. Scheduling is done so that athletes will miss a minimum amount of classroom time.   1 2 3 4 5 6 7

7. Scheduling is done so that as many games as possible can be played on the same date and trip (frosh, B team, varsity).   1 2 3 4 5 6 7

8. Scheduling is developed on the basis of equitable competition.   1 2 3 4 5 6 7

9. All game arrangements: date, time, place, etc., are taken care of with adequate advance notice.   1 2 3 4 5 6 7

10. The head coach participates in the scheduling of contests for the sport.   1 2 3 4 5 6 7

11. Efforts are made to keep the overlapping of seasonal scheduling at a minimum.   1 2 3 4 5 6 7

12. Competitive schedules of the sport are well advertised.   1 2 3 4 5 6 7

(continued on the next page)

13. The number of contests scheduled in the sport is in accordance with state association and/or national rules and regulations.	1	2	3	4	5	6	7
14. The number of scheduled contests is within the financial capabilities of the school.	1	2	3	4	5	6	7
C. Transportation	1	2	3	4	5	6	7

Comments

1. There is a clearly written policy regarding how to request transportation.	1	2	3	4	5	6	7
2. There are clearly written policies regarding what type of transportation may be used to and from athletic contests (i.e., public carrier, school bus, private car).	1	2	3	4	5	6	7
3. Someone is designated the responsibility for double checking all transportation requests.	1	2	3	4	5	6	7
4. There are clearly written rules and regulations regarding student conduct on trips.	1	2	3	4	5	6	7
5. Legal implications concerning the transportation of athletes and other personnel are known and understood.	1	2	3	4	5	6	7
6. Transportation provided in the sport is equitable with other sports in the program.	1	2	3	4	5	6	7
D. Personnel	1	2	3	4	5	6	7

Comments

1. All coaching personnel meet standards of state and local certification requirements.	1	2	3	4	5	6	7
2. All coaches are duly qualified to coach the sport.	1	2	3	4	5	6	7
3. All coaches are selected who have values that are in accordance with the community standards of morality.	1	2	3	4	5	6	7
4. Whenever the sport needs more coaching personnel due to demand by the number of students turning out, sufficient personnel are obtained.	1	2	3	4	5	6	7
5. More levels of teams are organized and additional contests for these teams are scheduled whenever the number of students turning out for the sport demands it.	1	2	3	4	5	6	7
6. There is an adequate staff for the sport.	1	2	3	4	5	6	7
7. Nonteaching personnel utilized in the program comply with state and local regulations.	1	2	3	4	5	6	7
8. Nonteaching personnel are utilized effectively in the program.	1	2	3	4	5	6	7
9. All faculty privileges and benefits (tenure, etc.) are available to coaches in the sport.	1	2	3	4	5	6	7
10. All athletic personnel in the sport are supportive of other staff members and their programs.	1	2	3	4	5	6	7

(continued on the next page)

11. All athletic personnel in the sport are active members in the professional organizations related to their teaching and coaching areas.   1 2 3 4 5 6 7

12. All athletic personnel in the sport effectively perform their functions as faculty members (teaching, committees, etc.).   1 2 3 4 5 6 7

13. All athletic personnel in the sport carry the equivalent work load (teaching, administration, etc.) as all other faculty members.   1 2 3 4 5 6 7

14. All athletic personnel in the sport have a positive influence on the student-athlete.   1 2 3 4 5 6 7

15. All supporting personnel (student managers, scorekeepers, statisticians, etc.) are utilized effectively.   1 2 3 4 5 6 7

16. All coaches show respect for the letter and intent of all rules and regulations.   1 2 3 4 5 6 7

17. All coaches have respect for authority and follow the lines of authority.   1 2 3 4 5 6 7

18. All coaches exhibit good sportsmanship.   1 2 3 4 5 6 7

19. All coaches actively teach good sportsmanship.   1 2 3 4 5 6 7

20. All coaches show maturity and self-control in contests (with athletes, officials, news media, parents, etc.).   1 2 3 4 5 6 7

21. All coaches display a high respect for the human dignity of athletes, parents, news media, officials, other coaches.   1 2 3 4 5 6 7

22. All coaches show professionalism through attendance at in-service programs, clinics, and conventions.   1 2 3 4 5 6 7

23. Salaries for coaches in the sport are equitable to salaries of coaches in other sports in the athletic program.   1 2 3 4 5 6 7

24. All coaches are coaching the sport because of their commitment to and qualifications for coaching the sport and not just for a salary supplement.   1 2 3 4 5 6 7

25. All coaches in the sport emphasize the importance of academics.   1 2 3 4 5 6 7

26. Harmonious relations, mutual respect and cooperation exist between the members of the coaching staff of the sport.   1 2 3 4 5 6 7

E. Contest Management   1 2 3 4 5 6 7

Comments

1. All contests start on time.   1 2 3 4 5 6 7

2. The visiting team is contacted well in advance and informed in writing about game plans and procedures (date, time, parking of bus, special details, etc.).   1 2 3 4 5 6 7

3. Arrangements are made for supervisory personnel to be present at all home contests.   1 2 3 4 5 6 7

(continued on the next page)

ASSESSMENT OF A SPORT PROGRAM (continued)

4. There is a thorough, complete, written check list for game management.   1 2 3 4 5 6 7

5. The game management check list covers all pregame, game, and postgame responsibilities effectively.   1 2 3 4 5 6 7

6. All half-time entertainment is well planned in advance.   1 2 3 4 5 6 7

7. Officials are contacted and given all pertinent information about the game contest well in advance (site, date, time etc.)   1 2 3 4 5 6 7

8. Possible problem areas are anticipated and prepared for effectively (police, parking, extra ticket booths, etc.).   1 2 3 4 5 6 7

9. The visiting team is treated as a "guest" and given all due consideration.   1 2 3 4 5 6 7

10. Facilities and any special equipment (phones, walkie-talkies, blackboards, etc.) are comparable and available to the visiting team if available to the home team.   1 2 3 4 5 6 7

F. Relations with League and State Associations   1 2 3 4 5 6 7

Comments

1. The school is an active participating member of the state association.   1 2 3 4 5 6 7

2. All coaches are provided with a state association's handbook.   1 2 3 4 5 6 7

3. All coaches in the sport know and adhere to all state and national association's rules in the sport.   1 2 3 4 5 6 7

4. All coaches are provided with a copy of league rules and regulations.   1 2 3 4 5 6 7

5. The coaches adhere to all league rules and regulations.   1 2 3 4 5 6 7

6. All athletes are made aware of the rules and regulations of the state association and league pertinent to them.   1 2 3 4 5 6 7

G. Evaluation   1 2 3 4 5 6 7

Comments

1. The sport program is effectively and unbiasedly evaluated yearly by the administration.   1 2 3 4 5 6 7

2. The coaches are unbiasedly evaluated annually in writing by the administration.   1 2 3 4 5 6 7

3. The head coach makes a comprehensive written evaluation of all assistant coaches annually.   1 2 3 4 5 6 7

4. All coaches have the opportunity to evaluate the total athletic program and the administration of the total athletic program annually in written form.   1 2 3 4 5 6 7

5. All assistant coaches in the sport have the opportunity to evaluate the sport program in which they are coaching annually in written form.   1 2 3 4 5 6 7

179

(continued on the next page)

6. There is an effective method for students, athletes, and nonathletes, to evaluate the program annually. 1 2 3 4 5 6 7

7. There is an effective method for members of the community to evaluate the program annually. 1 2 3 4 5 6 7

8. There is an effective method of evaluating whether the goals and objectives of the program are being met. 1 2 3 4 5 6 7

9. There is an effective method for evaluation annually of all personnel involved in the program (managers, score-keepers, announcers, etc.). 1 2 3 4 5 6 7

10. The sport is considered valuable by the student body. 1 2 3 4 5 6 7

V. Student in the Sport Program

A. Participation (i.e., meeting needs of students) 1 2 3 4 5 6 7

Comments

1. The welfare of the student-athlete is placed above all other considerations in the program. 1 2 3 4 5 6 7

2. The program offers enough levels of competition to permit all interested students to participate. 1 2 3 4 5 6 7

3. All interested students have equitable opportunity to try out and participate. 1 2 3 4 5 6 7

4. The goals and objectives of the sport are made known to all students. 1 2 3 4 5 6 7

5. All students are required to have a complete physical examination before turning out for the sport. 1 2 3 4 5 6 7

6. Students have the opportunity to participate in the formulation of goals and objectives, policies, and rules and regulations of the sport. 1 2 3 4 5 6 7

7. Athletes are made aware of procedures in appealing an arbitrary decision on the part of a coach or administrator. 1 2 3 4 5 6 7

8. The student body is made to feel a part of the program. 1 2 3 4 5 6 7

9. The student body is considered first in opportunities to attend contests. 1 2 3 4 5 6 7

10. Insurance programs and options are made known to all athletes. 1 2 3 4 5 6 7

11. All athletes are required to have written permission from parents/guardians before they may turn out for the sport. 1 2 3 4 5 6 7

12. The individual athlete is being developed to his/her maximum potential (athletic ability). 1 2 3 4 5 6 7

13. Opportunities are available for individuals or teams who excel in the sport to attend district, regional, state and/or national contests. 1 2 3 4 5 6 7

14. The sport is fun for the participants. 1 2 3 4 5 6 7

181

(continued on the next page)

B. School Spirit   1 2 3 4 5 6 7
Comments

1. Objectives and values of the program are effectively communicated to the faculty and student body.   1 2 3 4 5 6 7

2. The student body feels that the team in the sport is their team.   1 2 3 4 5 6 7

3. All personnel in the sport assume roles of leadership and/or involvement in active support of other school programs (debate, music, etc.).   1 2 3 4 5 6 7

4. All coaching personnel in the sport have empathy for and work effectively with students who are not in the sport.   1 2 3 4 5 6 7

5. All coaches in the sport respect and support other departments' programs.   1 2 3 4 5 6 7

6. All athletes in the sport are held to the same level of scholastic performance as other students.   1 2 3 4 5 6 7

7. All athletes in the sport are required to attend school and classes on the days of contests.   1 2 3 4 5 6 7

8. The sport serves as a rallying point, focus for loyalty and pride for the student body.   1 2 3 4 5 6 7

9. The sport serves as a rallying point, focus for loyalty and pride for the community   1 2 3 4 5 6 7

C. Awards   1 2 3 4 5 6 7
Comments

1. There is an awards presentation at the end of the season for all athletes in the sport.   1 2 3 4 5 6 7

2. Parents and community members are invited to the awards presentation.   1 2 3 4 5 6 7

3. Nonparticipating students are invited to the awards presentation.   1 2 3 4 5 6 7

4. All awards given in the sport are the same awards that all other sports in the program give to athletes.   1 2 3 4 5 6 7

5. Only the awards that are authorized by national or state associations, league rules, or school policy are given to athletes in the sport.   1 2 3 4 5 6 7

6. The coach helps the administration and other coaches plan the award system.   1 2 3 4 5 6 7

7. Outside groups (boosters, etc.) are discouraged from giving awards to athletes except through proper channels.   1 2 3 4 5 6 7

D. Health Considerations   1 2 3 4 5 6
Comments

1. A physician is in attendance at all appropriate contests.   1 2 3 4 5 6 7

2. Arrangements are made to have medical service available at all practices and game situations if appropriate.   1 2 3 4 5 6 7

183

(continued on the next page)

3. All coaches are required to have first aid certificates. 1 2 3 4 5 6 7

4. All athletes are required to have a health insurance policy before being allowed to participate. 1 2 3 4 5 6 7

5. All athletes are required to take a physical examination before turning out for the sport. 1 2 3 4 5 6 7

6. All facilities used in the sport are checked periodically to make certain they meet fire and safety requirements. 1 2 3 4 5 6 7

7. Lighting in the sport facilities meets at least minimum requirements. 1 2 3 4 5 6 7

8. All playing areas used in the sport are periodically checked to provide maximum safety. 1 2 3 4 5 6 7

9. There is a clearly written district procedure for coaches to follow in case of serious injury to an athlete. 1 2 3 4 5 6 7

10. There is a sufficient amount of practice time provided to properly condition and train athletes before participation in contests. 1 2 3 4 5 6 7

11. All playing surfaces are properly marked and finished to provide maximum safety. 1 2 3 4 5 6 7

12. Daily laundry of all practice apparel is provided by the school (socks, T-shirts, practice jerseys, etc.). 1 2 3 4 5 6 7

13. If daily laundry service is not provided by the school, there is an effective policy that aids students in keeping apparel clean. 1 2 3 4 5 6 7

14. Cleaning/laundry service is provided for contest apparel (uniforms, etc.). 1 2 3 4 5 6 7

15. If cleaning/laundry service is not provided by the school for contest apparel, there is an effective policy that aids students in keeping contest apparel clean. 1 2 3 4 5 6 7

E. Student Aid 1 2 3 4 5 6 7
Comments

1. Provisions and/or alternatives are provided for those athletes who cannot afford athletic fees (i.e., laundry fees, physical exams, etc.). 1 2 3 4 5 6 7

2. Provisions and/or alternatives are provided for those students who cannot afford athletic equipment normally provided by the athlete (shoes, socks, etc.). 1 2 3 4 5 6 7

3. The administration and coach make certain that athletes are not given special privileges that are not given to the entire student body. 1 2 3 4 5 6 7

Evaluation of Legal Aspects in Sports

This evaluation instrument consists of four major categories that are identified by Roman numerals. Within each major category there are varying numbers of subcategories that are identified by capital letters. *These are the ratings we are interested in.* To the right of each subcategory heading you will find a scale from 1–7. After you have examined the statements listed under each subcategory, circle the number for the subcategory that best represents your opinion of that area. The numerous statements (listed by Arabic numerals) are used merely as an aid to help you make a better evaluation of the subcategory rating. These statements also have the 1–7 scale and, in addition, some may be answered No or YES (if the response is NO circle 1, if the response is YES circle 7). The individual statements ratings can be "eyeballed" to determine the subcategory rating or the statements rated can be added and divided by the number of items rated (N) to determine an average subcategory rating. There may be statements that *do not apply* to your situation or *demand information not available* to you. If this is true, simply *omit responding* to those items. Add any additional comments in the left-hand margin.

EXAMPLE:

IV. Records and Information on Athletes

A. Health Records   1   2   3   ④   5   6   7
Comments

   1. Preseason physical examination data are kept on all athletes.   1   2   3   4   5   ⑥   7

   2. Accurate records of injuries occurring during practice and contests are kept on all athletes.   1   2   3   ④   5   6   7

   3. A written record of all medical treatment given to athletes is kept on file.   1   ②   3   4   5   6   7

Approximate visually or add numbers and divide by N for subcategory rating (i.e., $12 \div 3 = 4$).

Assessment of Legal Aspects in Sports

I. General Liability

A. Insurance   1 2 3 4 5 6 7
Comments

  1. The school has a good comprehensive plan for insurance: 1 2 3 4 5 6 7
    a. to protect institution.   1 2 3 4 5 6 7
    b. to protect officers, agents.   1 2 3 4 5 6 7
    c. to protect students, athletes.   1 2 3 4 5 6 7
  2. The school has a good legal advisor for insurance matters.   1 2 3 4 5 6 7
  3. The staff knows the difference between the two basic types of insurance, i.e., liability and accidental.   1 2 3 4 5 6 7
  4. All student assistants are covered by liability and accidental insurance.   1 2 3 4 5 6 7
  5. The staff is aware of the policy governing procedures for obtaining various kinds of insurance.   1 2 3 4 5 6 7
  6. The dollar amounts of insurance coverage are adequate and coverages are kept up-to-date.   1 2 3 4 5 6 7
  7. Arrangements are made for insurance coverage for use of facilities by nonstudent groups.   1 2 3 4 5 6 7

B. Classification and Association Relations   1 2 3 4 5 6 7
Comments

  1. All coaches are aware of the state rules governing participation in summer sports camps.   1 2 3 4 5 6 7
  2. All coaches are aware of which state athletic association rules are legally binding and which are recommendations.   1 2 3 4 5 6 7
  3. All eligibility standards established by governing associations are adhered to.   1 2 3 4 5 6 7
  4. Clear rules defining the "legal residence" of a student-athlete have been developed and published for the information of all.   1 2 3 4 5 6 7
  5. All coaches are aware of the legality of married students participating in sports.   1 2 3 4 5 6 7
  6. All coaches are knowledgeable about the legal guidelines enabling boys and girls to compete on the same team.   1 2 3 4 5 6 7

C. Standard of Care (If one is not qualified to act within a specific field, he/she should not attempt to do so.)   1 2 3 4 5 6 7
Comments

  1. Coaches use proper sequential coaching methods before intense competition or participation is permitted.   1 2 3 4 5 6 7

189

(continued on the next page)

2. Competent supervisors are assigned to conduct and/ or supervise practice in the absence of the coach. 1 2 3 4 5 6 7

3. Adequate supervision is always provided during practice and contests. 1 2 3 4 5 6 7

4. Special supervision is provided for less qualified and less experienced coaches until they become more qualified. 1 2 3 4 5 6 7

5. Sports administrators realize that if they assign un- qualified personnel to conduct an activity they may be held liable. 1 2 3 4 5 6 7

D. Transportation 1 2 3 4 5 6 7

Comments

1. All coaching personnel are aware of the liabilities involved in using public funds for transporting ath- letes to contests. 1 2 3 4 5 6 7

2. All coaching personnel are aware of the liabilities in- volved in allowing students to travel to athletic contests in private vehicles. 1 2 3 4 5 6 7

3. School owned motor vehicles or public utilities com- missioned licensees are used for transporting ath- letes and associated groups at all times. 1 2 3 4 5 6 7

4. All coaching personnel are aware of the liabilities in- volved in allowing students to drive their own ve- hicles to athletic contests. 1 2 3 4 5 6 7

5. All coaching personnel are aware that all drivers of private vehicles transporting athletes must possess valid licenses and appropriate insurance. 1 2 3 4 5 6 7

6. All coaching personnel exercise prudent judgment related to the loading of private vehicles carrying athletes. 1 2 3 4 5 6 7

7. All coaching personnel make certain private vehicles used for transporting athletes are checked to assure that they are in good safe working order. 1 2 3 4 5 6 7

8. A clearly written school policy is established relat- ing to team members going to and returning from contests as a team. 1 2 3 4 5 6 7

9. The school policy relating to team members going to and returning from contests as a team is adhered to by all coaching personnel. 1 2 3 4 5 6 7

E. Spectators 1 2 3 4 5 6 7

Comments

1. Spectators are reasonably protected from flying balls, bats, javelins, shots, etc. 1 2 3 4 5 6 7

2. Bleacher seats, steps, and railings are kept in good maintenance. 1 2 3 4 5 6 7

3. Potential damages to spectators at contests are anti- cipated and preventative measures taken. 1 2 3 4 5 6 7

(*continued on the next page*)

F. Supervision   1 2 3 4 5 6 7
Comments

1. Administrators effectively supervise athletic programs as well as academic subjects.   1 2 3 4 5 6 7
2. Good written policies are established prohibiting unsupervised athletic practice sessions.   1 2 3 4 5 6 7
3. The number of supervisors during practice and contests is appropriate for the number of participants and kind of activity.   1 2 3 4 5 6 7
4. All athletic contests involving physical contact are scheduled on the basis of equitable competition in regard to size, skill, etc.   1 2 3 4 5 6 7
5. Well-written rules are established for conducting safe lettermen club initiations.   1 2 3 4 5 6 7

G. Miscellaneous   1 2 3 4 5 6 7
Comments

1. The athletic director is clearly aware of legal precedence available or clear laws established on who has the "rights" to broadcast or telecast a sports contest.   1 2 3 4 5 6 7
2. All coaches are aware of situations resulting from personal exchanges that could result in law suits relating to libel and slander.   1 2 3 4 5 6 7
3. All coaching personnel are aware of the legality of purchasing athletic awards with public money.   1 2 3 4 5 6 7
4. All training rules, rules of social conduct, and dress standards are reasonable, prudent, and published for the information of all.   1 2 3 4 5 6 7
5. All coaching personnel are familiar with tort (negligence) liability as it relates to their coaching responsibilities.   1 2 3 4 5 6 7
6. All athletic personnel are aware of the Doctrine of Governmental Immunity as it applies to their state (at present approximately one half of the states have this law).   1 2 3 4 5 6 7

II. Equipment and Facilities

A. Equipment   1 2 3 4 5 6 7
Comments

1. Coaches make sure that protective equipment is kept in good condition.   1 2 3 4 5 6 7
2. Coaches refrain from "handing down" worn or defective equipment to junior varsity, freshman, and junior high teams.   1 2 3 4 5 6 7

193

(*continued on the next page*)

3. All coaches are aware that they are liable if rules that specify the use of protective equipment such as a mouthpiece, pads, helmets, etc. are not adhered to.
   1 2 3 4 5 6 7

4. All coaches regularly examine equipment used in contests such as bats, sticks, racquets, etc. to be sure they are free from defects that could cause injuries.
   1 2 3 4 5 6 7

5. All coaches use appropriate funds to purchase sports equipment.
   1 2 3 4 5 6 7

6. Coaches know how to order protective equipment that will be reliable.
   1 2 3 4 5 6 7

7. All coaches are aware of the legality of accepting gifts from sporting goods companies.
   1 2 3 4 5 6 7

8. Provisions are made to properly fit protective wearing apparel.
   1 2 3 4 5 6 7

9. Movable bleachers are designed effectively so that they cannot be tipped over.
   1 2 3 4 5 6 7

10. All coaches are aware that an athlete is not responsible for knowing necessary kinds of protective equipment needed or whether equipment is properly fitted or in safe condition.
    1 2 3 4 5 6 7

B. Facilities
   1 2 3 4 5 6 7

Comments

1. Coaches regularly consider potential dangers to students because of inadequate facilities.
   1 2 3 4 5 6 7

2. "Natural hazards" around playing fields (guy wires, poles, sprinkler holes, sharp corners, etc.) are considered regularly and protective padding and/or color coding is provided.
   1 2 3 4 5 6 7

3. Potential indoor hazards such as hard walls, radiators, slick floors, glass windows, fire extinguishers, etc., are considered in order to prevent the possibility of injury.
   1 2 3 4 5 6 7

4. Facilities considered as "attractive nuisances" (gymnastics area, swimming pools, etc.) are carefully supervised and kept locked when not being used.
   1 2 3 4 5 6 7

5. Periodic inspections related to maintenance of sports facilities are conducted (i.e., considering such items as electrical connections, dirty floors, faulty bleachers, fungus growth, etc.).
   1 2 3 4 5 6 7

6. A clear written policy has established who is responsible for inspection and maintenance of safe sports facilities (indoors and outdoors).
   1 2 3 4 5 6 7

195

(*continued on the next page*)

III. Medical Aspects							

A. Legal Considerations—Preseason 　　1 2 3 4 5 6 7
Comments

1. All coaches realize the legal implications of giving athletes food or dietary supplements. 　1 2 3 4 5 6 7

2. Coaches regularly confer with medical personnel regarding prevention of athletic injuries. 　1 2 3 4 5 6 7

3. All coaches use prudent judgment in permitting athletes with varying size and abilities to compete against one another. 　1 2 3 4 5 6 7

4. All coaches use reasonable judgment in advising athletes to gain or lose weight. 　1 2 3 4 5 6 7

5. All coaches demand a physical examination at the beginning of the season for any sport. 　1 2 3 4 5 6 7

6. All coaches have the ability to recognize symptoms that indicate injury. 　1 2 3 4 5 6 7

7. All coaches keep accurate records of injuries occurring during practices and contests. 　1 2 3 4 5 6 7

8. All coaches have proper and up-to-date first aid training. 　1 2 3 4 5 6 7

9. All coaches know the health status of the participants in their sport. 　1 2 3 4 5 6 7

B. Legal Considerations—During Seasons 　1 2 3 4 5 6 7
Comments

1. All coaches refrain from administering dietary supplements. 　1 2 3 4 5 6 7

2. All coaches use reasonable and prudent judgment in emergency situations. 　1 2 3 4 5 6 7

3. All coaches refrain from diagnosing injuries and illnesses. 　1 2 3 4 5 6 7

4. All coaches have medical assistance at all contact sports events and other sports when necessary. 　1 2 3 4 5 6 7

5. All coaches know when to apply first aid and when to seek medical aid. 　1 2 3 4 5 6 7

6. All coaches have medical assistance readily available during practice sessions. 　1 2 3 4 5 6 7

7. Clearly written policies and procedures have been established to be followed in treating injuries occurring during practices and/or contests. 　1 2 3 4 5 6 7 / 1 2 3 4 5 6 7

8. All coaches use sound sequential conditioning procedures throughout the season. 　1 2 3 4 5 6 7

C. Legal Considerations—Postcontest or Postseason 　1 2 3 4 5 6 7
Comment

1. All coaches secure medical approval for any treatment prescribed, i.e., diathermy, x-rays, etc. 　1 2 3 4 5 6 7

2. All coaches require written medical approval for further participation after illness or injury. 　1 2 3 4 5 6 7

197

(continued on the next page)

IV. Records and Information on Athletes							

	1	2	3	4	5	6	7
A. Health Records	1	2	3	4	5	6	7
Comments							
1. Preseason physical examination data are kept on all athletes.	1	2	3	4	5	6	7
2. Accurate records of injuries occurring during practices and contests are kept on all athletes.	1	2	3	4	5	6	7
3. A written record on all medical treatment given to athletes is kept on file.	1	2	3	4	5	6	7
4. Written permission by a physician, which allows an injured athlete to reenter competition, is kept on file.	1	2	3	4	5	6	7
B. Documents from Parents	1	2	3	4	5	6	7
Comments							
1. A written letter of consent from parents that allows a student to participate in athletics is kept on file.	1	2	3	4	5	6	7
2. A copy of the athlete's birth certificate is kept on file to verify birthdate.	1	2	3	4	5	6	7
3. Letters from parents requesting that athletes return from athletic trips by means other than official school carriers are required and kept on file.	1	2	3	4	5	6	7
4. Written permission by a parent and/or physician that allows an athlete who has been ill to reenter competition is kept on file.	1	2	3	4	5	6	7
C. Assessment of Performance	1	2	3	4	5	6	7
Comments							
1. Written evaluations of the athlete's character or physical abilities are open and accessible to the athlete.	1	2	3	4	5	6	7

Athletic Facilities Evaluation Instrument *

The Athletic Facilities Evaluation Instrument is designed to aid the evaluator in assessing the facility. Much insight can also be gained by personally talking to student-athletes, coaches, custodians, and administrative personnel regarding the soundness of the facility. The profile and the scoring system used in this instrument is slightly different from others used in this manual; therefore a special explanation is given for this instrument.

ORGANIZATIONAL STRUCTURE USED

The Athletic Facilities Evaluation Instrument utilizes the system where the middle school (MS) includes grades 5–8, the high school (HS) includes grades 9–12, and the community college (CC) includes grades 13 and 14. This seems to be the best organizational pattern as far as athletic facilities are concerned where their use must be integrated with other physical education programs. Since colleges can range in size from a few hundred to many thousand students, the CC rating and profile should be used for rating college facilities.

AREA DESCRIPTIONS

The critique instrument consists of thirteen areas. The areas are numbered for reference and, in addition, a verbal description is given. The *LEVEL* column provides spaces with·checks indicating whether the item is applicable for that level of the schools. The *RATING* column provides space for the evaluator to mark his rating (based upon subjective judgment) about how well that item has been given consideration. If the item is not present, a zero would be entered or the space left blank. A rating of one indicates *present but poor,* a rating of two represents *average,* and a rating of three should be given for a *good feature.* The remarks column is available for indication of such things as: the kind of lighting, the color of walls, the color of court markings, the width of court lines, voltage of electrical outlets, etc.

TOTAL AREA RATINGS

After each area has been evaluated, the rating column is accumulated to determine the total. At the bottom of each area is a number indicating the total number of points possible for each level. The total for each area will later be plotted on the Profile. No attempt has been made to "weight" the areas as to relative importance. Each area will be evaluated on the Profile independently as a percentage of the total number of points possible. All features of an area cannot be anticipated. Unique features in any area are worth noting even though they are not included on the Instrument. Provision has been made for a maximum of two additional area items deemed important to the evaluation (a maximum of six bonus points per area). If these items are present, add them to the list and rate them. The total

*Adapted from: Penman, *Planning Physical Education and Athletic Facilities in Schools.* Copyright 1977 John Wiley and Sons. Used with permission.

possible number of points for each area equals the number of items checked in the level column times the maximum rating for each item (three).

COMBINED AREAS

Occasionally it will be necessary to combine areas. For example, a high school may have a training area in the locker room, the weight training area may be in the multipurpose room, etc. Whenever possible, for evaluation purposes, these areas should be evaluated independently even though they are in the same area. Note under the remarks column any undesirable situations this may present, e.g., wastes half the space of the room, provides insufficient teaching stations, etc.

DUPLICATED AREAS

In some instances an area may be duplicated several times. For example, there may be two baseball diamonds and four softball diamonds. In this case, under "no. of diamonds" the evaluator must subjectively determine under the conditions of the specific school: the number of baseball and softball programs in operation, amount of time during the day they are available, other field space available, etc. If there are a sufficient number of diamonds a rating of two or three would be given.

DIFFERENCES IN BOYS' AND GIRLS' FACILITIES

In general, athletic facilities are asexual. That is, a good facility (field, court, locker, storage bin, etc.) is independent of differing sex. To be sure, there are special considerations necessary regarding such things as height of shower heads, relative number of showers, team rooms, visiting team areas, etc. However, in evaluating a facility, these differences are noted in the remarks column. When considering men's and women's offices, show rooms, locker rooms, etc., a biological symbol separates the rating column so that similar areas may be compared on the same sheet.

THE PROFILE

After each area in the facility has been evaluated, the rating column should be totaled. The Profiles found in Chapter 3 list each area. There are three profiles for different levels of education. A horizontal line on the profile indicates the total number of possible points for each area. A heavier line indicates the upper 20 percent of the total possible number of points. Enter the total number of points for each area on the profile by placing a dot on each horizontal line. If the area was nonexistent, enter a dot at zero. When all dots have been entered, a line can be made connecting the dots to form the profile of the school athletic facilities. A sample completed profile is shown for a community college in Figure 6.

EFFICIENCY RATING

The efficiency rating of 80 percent or above has been indicated on the profile as being satisfactory. This percentage of the total possible number of points is purely arbitrary and based upon the philosophy that if a facility does not include 80 percent of what should be there, it is inadequate. The ultimate decision as to what standard will be used to judge the facility will be determined by the school officials.

The Instrument is used merely as an aid to evaluating a facility. Each area in the facility can be examined to determine how good it is by examining where the point lies on each vertical line in relation to the acceptable limits. The profile shows how the overall facility fares by examining how many and which areas are above the 80 percent lines.

The following instruments are *examples* of evaluation forms that can be used.

Figure 6

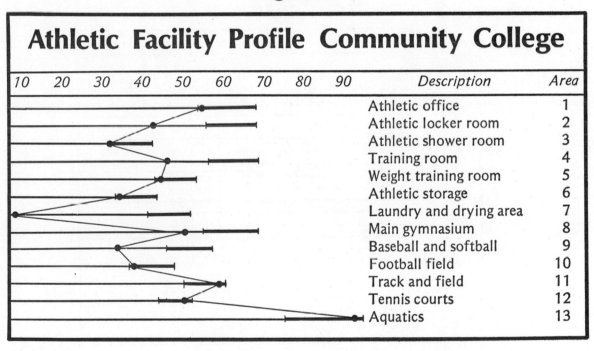

Athletic Facility Profile Community College		
10 20 30 40 50 60 70 80 90	*Description*	*Area*
	Athletic office	1
	Athletic locker room	2
	Athletic shower room	3
	Training room	4
	Weight training room	5
	Athletic storage	6
	Laundry and drying area	7
	Main gymnasium	8
	Baseball and softball	9
	Football field	10
	Track and field	11
	Tennis courts	12
	Aquatics	13

Facility Evaluation

Educational Level Requirement	Area _____ No. ____	Rating 1-2-3 ♂	Rating 1-2-3 ♀	Additional Remarks
This column need not be checked. From each specific evaluation sheet select the appropriate educational level (i.e. MS, HS or CC) and transfer the items listed for the selected level to this sheet.				

Total possible points = the number of items listed times the maximum rating for each item (three).

Total Points

(continued on the next page)

Adapted from: Penman, *Planning Physical Education and Athletic Facilities in Schools.* Copyright 1977 John Wiley and Sons. Used with permission.

FACILITY EVALUATION (*continued*)

Level			Area 1	Rating		Remarks
				1–2–3		
MS	HS	CC	Athletic Office	♂	♀	
X	X		visibility to lockers			
X	X	X	acoustics			
X	X	X	aesthetics			
X	X	X	tele. outside line			
X	X	X	tele. inside line			
X	X	X	no. of desk spaces			
X	X	X	bulletin boards			
X	X	X	chalkboards			
X	X	X	master H_2O temp. cont.			
X	X	X	lighting			
X	X	X	clock			
X	X	X	climate control			
X	X	X	elect. outlets l/wall			
X	X	X	floor surface approp.			
X	X	X	storage – shelves, etc.			
	X	X	film review area			
			locker room:			
			adequate no. of lockers			
X	X	X	for all coaches			
X	X	X	showers			
X	X	X	wc and urinals			
X	X	X	lavatory			
X	X	X	mirror			
X	X	X	bench and/or chairs			
X	X	X	refrigerator			

Total possible points
66
69
66

Total Points

(continued on the next page)

Adapted from: Penman, *Planning Physical Education and Athletic Facilities in Schools.* Copyright 1977 John Wiley and Sons. Used with permission.

FACILITY EVALUATION (*continued*)

	Level		Area 2	Rating		Remarks
MS	HS	CC	Athletic Locker Room	♂	♀	
?	X	X	full size airy lockers			
	X	X	open space around lockers			
	X	X	flex for diff. sports			
	X	X	lighting protected			
	X	X	drainage			
	X	X	bulletin board			
	X	X	chalkboard			
	X	X	exhaust fans			
	X	X	benches			
	X	X	drinking fountain			
	X	X	clock protected			
	X	X	floor surface adeq.			
	X	X	aesthetics			
	X	X	mirrors			
	X	X	acoustics			
	X	X	hose connection			
	X	X	traffic pattern			
	X	X	hose down area			
	X	X	movie screen or wall			
	X	X	towel storage			
			rest rooms:			
	X	X	adeq. no. of lavs.			
			adeq. no. of wc and			
	X	X	urinals			
	X	X	adeq. no. of mirrors			

Total possible points
— 69
— 69

Total Points

(continued on the next page)

Adapted from: Penman, *Planning Physical Education and Athletic Facilities in Schools.* Copyright 1977 John Wiley and Sons. Used with permission.

Level			Area 3	Rating		
				1–2–3		
MS	*HS*	*CC*	*Athletic Shower Room*	♂	♀	*Remarks*
?	X	X	shower head layout			
	X	X	shower control – indiv.			
	X	X	walls and corners			
	X	X	floor surface			
	X	X	lighting			
	X	X	urinal			
	X	X	soap dispensers			
			drying area			
	X	X	floor surface			
	X	X	drainage			
	X	X	towel issue layout			
	X	X	absence of glass			
	X	X	floor drains			
	X	X	aesthetics			
	X	X	hose connection			

Total possible points
42
42

Total Points

(continued on the next page)

Adapted from: Penman, *Planning Physical Education and Athletic Facilities in Schools.* Copyright 1977 John Wiley and Sons. Used with permission.

FACILITY EVALUATION (*continued*)

Level			Area 4	Rating		Remarks
MS	HS	CC	Training Room	1–2–3		
				♂	♀	
?	X	X	tables and benches			
	X	X	elec. out. 110 + 220			
	X	X	sink counter space			
	X	X	med. supply cabinets			
	X	X	lighting			
	X	X	climate control			
	X	X	bulletin board			
	X	X	refrigerator			
	X	X	whirlpool			
	X	X	heat lamps, etc.			
	X	X	mirrors			
	X	X	floor surface			
	X	X	aesthetics			
	X	X	acoustics			
		X	ice maker			
			doctor's exam room:			
		X	table			
		X	lamp minor surg.			
		X	cab. surg. supply			
		X	office doctor/trainer			
			rest room:			
		X	wc			
		X	lavatory			
		X	shower			
	X	X	accessible to both sexes			
			Total possible points	Total Points		
			69			
			45			

(continued on the next page)

Adapted from: Penman, *Planning Physical Education and Athletic Facilities in Schools.* Copyright 1977 John Wiley and Sons. Used with permission.

FACILITY EVALUATION (continued)

Level			Area 5	Rating		
				1–2–3		
MS	HS	CC	Weight Training Room	♂	♀	Remarks
?	X	X	lighting			
	X	X	acoustics			
	X	X	aesthetics			
	X	X	climate control			
	X	X	mirrors			
	X	X	floor surface			
		X	lifting platform			
	X	X	weight storage racks			
	X	X	barbells—fixed			
		X	barbells—adj.			
	X	X	dumbbells			
	X	X	multi-station machine			
	X	X	isometric stations			
	X	X	incline boards			
	X	X	benches			
	X	X	various racks			
	X	X	bulletin board			

Total possible points
51
45

Total Points

(continued on the next page)

FACILITY EVALUATION (*continued*)

MS	HS	CC	Area 6 — Athletic Storage	Rating 1–2–3 ♂	♀	Remarks
			approp. locations			
			outdoor:			
X	X	X	jumping pits			
X	X	X	standards			
X	X	X	cross bars			
X	X	X	dummies			
			indoor:			
X	X	X	apparatus—tramp.			
X	X	X	uniforms			
X	X	X	shoes, pads, helmets			
X	X	X	daily equipment			
X	X	X	off-season equip.			
X	X	X	accessibility			
X	X	X	lighting—protected			
X	X	X	climate control			
X	X	X	elect. outlets			
X	X	X	safe ladder or stool			

Total possible points
— 42
— 42
— 42

Total Points

(continued on the next page)

Adapted from: Penman, *Planning Physical Education and Athletic Facilities in Schools.* Copyright 1977 John Wiley and Sons. Used with permission.

Level			Area 7	Rating		
				1–2–3		
MS	HS	CC	*Laundry and Drying Area*	♂	♀	*Remarks*
			Laundry area:			
	X	X	lighting			
	X	X	climate control			
	X	X	special venting			
	X		washer			
	X	X	dryer			
		X	washer-extractor			
	X	X	storage area for			
			soap etc.			
	X	X	elect. out. 110–220			
	X	X	sloping floor			
	X	X	floor drain			
	X	X	folding table			
	X	X	clean towel and			
			uniform storage bins			
			drying area:			
X	X	X	lighting			
X	X	X	climate control			
X	X	X	special venting			
X	X	X	sloping floor			
X	X	X	floor drain			
X	X	X	hose outlet			

Total possible points
51
51
18

Total Points

(*continued on the next page*)

Adapted from: Penman, *Planning Physical Education and Athletic Facilities in Schools.* Copyright 1977 John Wiley and Sons. Used with permission.

FACILITY EVALUATION (*continued*)

Level			Area 8	Rating		Remarks
				1-2-3		
MS	*HS*	*CC*	*Main Gym*	♂	♀	*Remarks*
X	X	X	bleachers flush fold			
X	X	X	acoustics			
X	X	X	aesthetics			
X	X	X	recessed drink. fount.			
X	X	X	recessed cuspidor			
X	X	X	min. one clear wall			
X	X	X	lighting height			
X	X	X	chalkboard—flush mtg.			
X	X	X	backboards elect.			
X	X	X	backboards glass in			
			front of spectators			
X	X	X	scoreboard			
X	X	X	PA and AV system			
	X	X	press-radio area			
X	X	X	clock			
			floor markings:			
X	X	X	approp. colors			
X	X	X	approp. width			
X	X	X	elect. outlets			
X	X	X	flexibility			
X	X	X	absence of safety haz.			
X	X	X	climate control			
X	X	X	adeq. ventilation			
X	X	X	floor plates for appar.			
X	X	X	storage large doors			

Total possible points
— 69
— 69
— 66

Total Points

(continued on the next page)

Adapted from: Penman, *Planning Physical Education and Athletic Facilities in Schools.* Copyright 1977 John Wiley and Sons. Used with permission.

FACILITY EVALUATION (*continued*)

Level			Area 9	Rating		Remarks
				1-2-3		
MS	HS	CC	*Baseball Softball*	♂	♀	
			baseball area:			
X	X		300 × 300 ft.			
		X	400 × 400 ft.			
X	X	X	backstop			
X	X	X	bleachers			
	X	X	player benches			
X	X	X	compass direction			
		X	lights			
X	X	X	drinking fountain			
	X	X	elect. outlets			
X	X	X	watering system			
X	X	X	scoreboard			
X	X	X	storage			
	X	X	no. of fields			
X	X	X	fences			
			softball area:			
X			150 × 150 ft.			
	X		200 × 200 ft.			
		X	275 × 275 ft.			
X	X	X	backstop			
X	X	X	player benches			
X	X	X	compass direction			
X	X	X	no. of fields			

Total possible points
54
51
42

Total Points

(continued on the next page)

Adapted from: Penman, *Planning Physical Education and Athletic Facilities in Schools*. Copyright 1977 John Wiley and Sons. Used with permission.

FACILITY EVALUATION (*continued*)

Level			Area 10	Rating		Remarks
				1–2–3		
MS	HS	CC	Football Field	♂	♀	
	X	X	bleachers direction			
	X	X	press box			
	X	X	lighting			
	X	X	electric outlets			
X	X	X	scoreboard			
X	X	X	drinking fountain			
			turf:			
X	X	X	kind			
X	X	X	condition			
X	X	X	crown			
X	X	X	drainage			
X	X	X	watering method			
X	X	X	goal posts			
X	X	X	fence and gates			
X	X	X	side line markers			
X	X	X	compass direction			

Total possible points
— 45
— 45
— 33

Total Points

(*continued on the next page*)

Adapted from: Penman, *Planning Physical Education and Athletic Facilities in Schools.* Copyright 1977 John Wiley and Sons. Used with permission.

214

FACILITY EVALUATION (*continued*)

Level			Area 11	Rating		
				1–2–3		
MS	HS	CC	*Track and Field*	♂	♀	*Remarks*
			tracks:			
X	X	X	surface composition			
X	X	X	surface condition			
X	X	X	no. of lanes			
X	X	X	length of track			
X	X	X	lane markings			
X	X	X	curbs			
X	X	X	distances marked			
X	X	X	drainage			
		X	judges stand			
			jumping pits:			
X	X	X	drainage			
X	X	X	runways			
X	X	X	standards			
X	X	X	pit composition			
X	X	X	compass direction			
			weight event areas:			
	X	X	shot put ring comp.			
	X	X	shot put landing			
			area composition			
	X	X	shot put kick board			
	X	X	discus ring comp.			
	X	X	discus ring kick bd.			
	X	X	bleachers			
			Total possible points		Total Points	
			60			
			57			
			39			

(*continued on the next page*)

Adapted from: Penman, *Planning Physical Education and Athletic Facilities in Schools*. Copyright 1977 John Wiley and Sons. Used with permission.

FACILITY EVALUATION (*continued*)

MS	HS	CC	Area 12 — Tennis Courts	Rating 1-2-3 ♂	♀	Remarks
?	X	X	no. of courts			
	X	X	surface composition			
	X	X	line markings			
	X	X	drainage			
	X	X	hose connection			
	X	X	fence			
	X	X	gates			
	X	X	drinking fountain			
	X	X	judges stand			
	X	X	storage of balls, mach.			
	X	X	volley wall			
		X	lights			
	X	X	elect. outlets			
	X	X	nets			
	X	X	posts			
	X	X	clearance around cts.			
	X	X	color of court			

Total possible points
51
48

Total Points

(continued on the next page)

Adapted from: Penman, *Planning Physical Education and Athletic Facilities in Schools.* Copyright 1977 John Wiley and Sons. Used with permission.

FACILITY EVALUATION (*continued*)

| Level | | | Area 13 | Rating | | |
| MS | HS | CC | | 1-2-3 | | |
			Aquatics	♂	♀	Remarks
X	X	X	dimensions			
X	X	X	range of depth			
X	X	X	composition of pool			
	X	X	underwater lights			
	X	X	underwater windows			
	X	X	lanes, width and no.			
	X	X	diving boards			
		X	diving platform			
X	X	X	lifeguard stations			
	X	X	deck dimensions			
	X	X	deck surface			
	X	X	deck drainage			
	X	X	gutters			
	X	X	hose connections			
	X	X	electrical outlets			
X	X	X	fence			
	X	X	recessed ladders			
	X	X	compass direction			
	X	X	drinking fountain			
	X	X	clock			
X	X	X	storage			
	X	X	concessions			
X	X	X	adeq. filter system			
	X	X	PA system			
	X	X	office supervision			
	X	X	climate cont. (indoor)			
	X	X	spectator area			
	X	X	lighting			

(continued on the next page)

Adapted from: Penman, *Planning Physical Education and Athletic Facilities in Schools.* Copyright 1977 John Wiley and Sons. Used with permission.

FACILITY EVALUATION (*continued*)

MS	HS	CC	Area 13 / Aquatics	♂	♀	Remarks
			Level / Rating 1–2–3			
	X	X	aesthetics			
	X	X	showers and lockers			
			rest rooms			
	X	X	clothes check system			
	X	X	acoustics (indoor pools)			

Total possible points
96
93
21

Total Points

Adapted from: Penman, *Planning Physical Education and Athletic Facilities in Schools.* Copyright 1977 John Wiley and Sons. Used with permission.

PART FOUR

Physical Education Program and Personnel Assessment Instruments

Directions for Evaluating
the Physical Education Chairperson

NAME _____

This evaluation instrument consists of three major categories that are identified by Roman numerals. Within each major category there are varying numbers of subcategories that are identified by capital letters. *These are the ratings we are interested in.* To the right of each subcategory heading you will find a scale from 1–7. After you have examined the statements listed under each subcategory, circle the number for the subcategory that best represents your opinion of that area. The numerous statements (listed by Arabic numerals) are used merely as an aid to help you make a better evaluation of the subcategory rating. These statements also have the 1–7 scale and, in addition, some may be answered NO or YES (if the response is NO circle 1, if the response is YES circle 7). The individual statements ratings can be "eyeballed" to determine the subcategory rating or the statements rated can be added and divided by the number of items rated (N) to determine an average subcategory rating. There may be statements that *do not apply* to your situation or *demand information not available* to you. If this is true, simply *omit responding* to those items. Add any additional comments in the left-hand margin.

EXAMPLE:

I. Personal Qualities	
A. Human Relations	1 2 3 ④ 5 6 7
Comments	
The administrator:	
1. gives recognition to good work.	1 2 ③ 4 5 6 7
2. is willing to put others first.	1 ② 3 4 5 6 7
3. lets staff and faculty know how they are doing a particular job or responsibility.	1 2 3 4 5 ⑥ 7
	Approximate visually or add numbers and divide by N for the subcategory rating (i.e. 11 ÷ 3 = 3.7).

Assessment of the
Physical Education Department Chairperson

I. Personal Qualities

    A. Human Relations   1 2 3 4 5 6 7

Comments

    The administrator:

1. gives recognition to good work.   1 2 3 4 5 6 7
2. is willing to put others first.   1 2 3 4 5 6 7
3. lets staff and faculty know how they are doing a particular job or responsibility (either positive or negative feedback).   1 2 3 4 5 6 7
4. maintains an open, positive working relationship with students.   1 2 3 4 5 6 7
5. treats faculty and staff humanely.   1 2 3 4 5 6 7
6. is objective in praising and criticizing.   1 2 3 4 5 6 7
7. helps create and maintain high morals.   1 2 3 4 5 6 7
8. is honest in conversations and decisions.   1 2 3 4 5 6 7
9. has the ability to adjust to varying levels of comprehension in conversations.   1 2 3 4 5 6 7
10. is friendly and approachable.   1 2 3 4 5 6 7
11. stimulates others to seek new ways of solving problems.   1 2 3 4 5 6 7
12. recognizes and accepts individual differences between associates.   1 2 3 4 5 6 7
13. shows trust in others.   1 2 3 4 5 6 7
14. recognizes others wish to succeed and encourages them toward success.   1 2 3 4 5 6 7

    B. Personality Traits   1 2 3 4 5 6 7

Comments

    The administrator:

1. expresses himself/herself well in relation to vocabulary, grammar, etc.   1 2 3 4 5 6 7
2. shows a keen and appropriate sense of humor.   1 2 3 4 5 6 7
3. has original and stimulating ideas and viewpoints.   1 2 3 4 5 6 7
4. is congenial in conversations and/or discussions.   1 2 3 4 5 6 7
5. is decisive and forceful when needed.   1 2 3 4 5 6 7
6. displays a hospitable and friendly attitude.   1 2 3 4 5 6 7
7. is consistent in behavior.   1 2 3 4 5 6 7
8. shows self-confidence and meets difficulties with poise.   1 2 3 4 5 6 7
9. has the ability to admit weaknesses and/or mistakes.   1 2 3 4 5 6 7
10. receives criticism without getting defensive.   1 2 3 4 5 6 7
11. has the desire to be successful in his/her job or work   1 2 3 4 5 6 7

223

(continued on the next page)

C. Physical Characteristics   1   2   3   4   5   6   7
Comments

   The administrator:

     1. presents an appearance representative of the position.   1   2   3   4   5   6   7

     2. exhibits substantial freedom from annoying or distracting personal mannerism.   1   2   3   4   5   6   7

II. Professional Growth

A. Personal Reading and Writing   1   2   3   4   5   6   7
Comments

   The administrator:

     1. keeps up-to-date by reading current publications (books, periodicals, journals) relative to administration.   1   2   3   4   5   6   7

     2. is active in conducting research relative to his/her duties.   1   2   3   4   5   6   7

     3. periodically publishes research relative to his/her specialty or role as an administrator.   1   2   3   4   5   6   7

B. Affiliation with Professional Associations   1   2   3   4   5   6   7
Comments

   The administrator:

     1. attends meetings and conferences with individuals, groups and/or organizations relative to his/her role as an administrator of the department.   1   2   3   4   5   6   7

     2. strives to improve his/her active participation in the organizations of which he/she is a member or by accepting positions of authority by volunteering time on committees, etc.   1   2   3   4   5   6   7

     3. represents himself/herself in a professional manner when attending conventions, meetings or conferences.   1   2   3   4   5   6   7

C. Professional Interaction   1   2   3   4   5   6   7
Comments

   The administrator:

     1. regularly makes new acquaintances in the field to discover different philosophies and ideas that may help improve the department or his/her role as an administrator.   1   2   3   4   5   6   7

     2. confers with other administrators in the field for advice, discussion, current developments, new leads, etc.   1   2   3   4   5   6   7

     3. represents the department to the school and community in a respectable and professional manner.   1   2   3   4   5   6   7

(*continued on the next page*)

III. Administrative Responsibilities

A. Organization   1 2 3 4 5 6 7
Comments
The administrator:
1. is aware of the dynamics of the organization.   1 2 3 4 5 6 7
2. holds staff meetings when necessary.   1 2 3 4 5 6 7
3. establishes priorities of duties and allocates time relative to their importance.   1 2 3 4 5 6 7
4. is effective in relation to the administration in the budget cycle.   1 2 3 4 5 6 7
5. sees that instructional courses are organized and supervised according to departmental policy and procedure.   1 2 3 4 5 6 7
6. has the ability to keep discussions relevant, uses proper rules of order, and allows freedom implied by the democratic process when conducting a meeting.   1 2 3 4 5 6 7
7. establishes policies and procedures upon a systematic accumulation and interpretation of facts.   1 2 3 4 5 6 7
8. uses normal daily hours for aiding instruction and office operation and leaves self-improvement and other office procedural tasks until a later hour.   1 2 3 4 5 6 7
9. realizes the importance of a clean, orderly, cheerful physical plant and environment.   1 2 3 4 5 6 7
10. has the ability to discern which problems need action by the department and those that are informative and can be distributed by memo.   1 2 3 4 5 6 7
11. develops and/or maintains a progressive, functioning program.   1 2 3 4 5 6 7
12. in the evaluative process with the faculty and staff members, determines those individuals to be dismissed and advises such individuals with reasons or intended recommendations.   1 2 3 4 5 6 7
13. effectively utilizes the committee system.   1 2 3 4 5 6 7
14. projects, with the faculty and assistance from central office, student enrollment and demographic descriptions of that enrollment.   1 2 3 4 5 6 7
15. efficient in organizing the department for effective and smooth operation.   1 2 3 4 5 6 7
16. develops processes for student elections of officers and representatives.   1 2 3 4 5 6 7
B. Communication Skills   1 2 3 4 5 6 7
Comments
The administrator:
1. communicates effectively with staff, faculty, and other personnel of the school.   1 2 3 4 5 6 7

227

(*continued on the next page*)

2. confers with the faculty individually and as a group   1   2   3   4   5   6   7
   to determine professional needs.
3. is effective in obtaining school support for the de-   1   2   3   4   5   6   7
   partment.
4. effectively maintains contact with alumni.   1   2   3   4   5   6   7
5. makes staff feel at ease when talking with them.   1   2   3   4   5   6   7
6. is easily understood.
7. conducts decisive conferences and interviews.   1   2   3   4   5   6   7
8. makes known publicly his/her desire to have a   1   2   3   4   5   6   7
   strong, representative student committee that is
   free to make decisions in its realm of jurisdiction.
9. shows understanding of the purposes and acceptable   1   2   3   4   5   6   7
   practices of guidance and counseling in relation to
   faculty-student interaction.
10. is effective in transaction of official departmental   1   2   3   4   5   6   7
    business with superiors.
11. is available to faculty, staff, and students for the   1   2   3   4   5   6   7
    purpose of ameliorating any problems and adjust-
    ing any differences (open-door policy).
12. finds time to listen to staff members.   1   2   3   4   5   6   7
13. is open to suggestions and ideas.   1   2   3   4   5   6   7
14. communicates in a timely and responsive manner.
15. makes clear the route of appeal in event of disagree-   1   2   3   4   5   6   7
    ment or conflict between staff members and su-
    periors.
16. holds meetings with faculty on a regular basis.   1   2   3   4   5   6   7
17. confers with individual faculty members through-   1   2   3   4   5   6   7
    out the academic year to assist in establishing ac-
    ceptable levels of professional performance.
18. maintains a good relationship toward other related   1   2   3   4   5   6   7
    departments (i.e., biology, computer science, busi-
    ness, health services, etc.).
19. follows through to make sure that communications   1   2   3   4   5   6   7
    are received and understood.
20. makes sure that his/her part in the organization is   1   2   3   4   5   6   7
    understood by all faculty and staff members.
21. has developed and maintains a good system for   1   2   3   4   5   6   7
    communication.
22. is duly sensitive to the staff's need for informa-   1   2   3   4   5   6   7
    tion.
23. is a good listener.   1   2   3   4   5   6   7
24. clearly states memos and letters.   1   2   3   4   5   6   7
25. distributes to faculty and staff in memorandum   1   2   3   4   5   6   7
    form, those decisions or announcements needing no
    discussion.

229

(*continued on the next page*)

26. before publishing tentative decisions in memorandum form, communicates those decisions to faculty meetings or conferences if the decisions require clarification or revision by these groups.   1 2 3 4 5 6 7

C. Leadership   1 2 3 4 5 6 7

Comments

The administrator:

1. carries out or implements decisions with firmness and dispatch.   1 2 3 4 5 6 7

2. is effective in distributing teaching and research loads.   1 2 3 4 5 6 7

3. crusades for what is in the best interests of the faculty and/or department, even though it may be unpopular with superiors.   1 2 3 4 5 6 7

4. gives ideas suggested by faculty and staff full consideration.   1 2 3 4 5 6 7

5. sees that department members effectively fulfill assigned responsibilities.   1 2 3 4 5 6 7

6. assumes a responsibility for doing things (like acquiring grants and publishing) which he/she requires of his/her subordinates.   1 2 3 4 5 6 7

7. effectively assigns responsibility and authority to department members and committees.   1 2 3 4 5 6 7

8. encourages professional growth of faculty.   1 2 3 4 5 6 7

9. observes the code of ethics of his/her professional organization.   1 2 3 4 5 6 7

D. Staff Relationships   1 2 3 4 5 6 7

Comments

The administrator

1. provides encouragement and direction to faculty and staff.   1 2 3 4 5 6 7

2. lets staff members know what is expected of them.   1 2 3 4 5 6 7

3. is effective as a liaison or conveyer of information between the departmental faculty and staff.   1 2 3 4 5 6 7

4. works to assist teachers in their professional performance in the classroom.   1 2 3 4 5 6 7

5. identifies in the evaluative process with the faculty and staff members, those individuals who should be reassigned or promoted with specific recommendations in each case.   1 2 3 4 5 6 7

6. fosters good teaching in the department.   1 2 3 4 5 6 7

7. is supportive of teacher classroom concerns.

8. respects the professional rights of faculty.   1 2 3 4 5 6 7

9. is effective in stimulating research by faculty.   1 2 3 4 5 6 7

10. supports the actions of staff members.   1 2 3 4 5 6 7

11. says "NO" effectively.   1 2 3 4 5 6 7

(*continued on the next page*)

12. is effective in identifying the abilities faculty/   1   2   3   4   5   6   7
staff members possess and provides the oppor-
tunities for them to be used to benefit the department.
13. criticizes poor work effectively and tactfully.   1   2   3   4   5   6   7
14. appraises staff, as nearly as possible, on the basis   1   2   3   4   5   6   7
of objective, measurable performance.
15. puts appropriate suggestions made by staff into   1   2   3   4   5   6   7
operation.
16. appoints effective committees.   1   2   3   4   5   6   7
17. follows evaluative processes suggested in the policy   1   2   3   4   5   6   7
adopted by the faculty manual.
18. is effective in making recommendations to the ad-   1   2   3   4   5   6   7
ministration for appointments, promotions, and
salaries for members of the department.
19. determines needs for improvement in the evaluative   1   2   3   4   5   6   7
process with faculty and staff members, and super-
vises activities toward improvement.

E. Planning and Foresight   1   2   3   4   5   6   7

Comments

The administrator:
1. has long-range plans that coincide with the objec-   1   2   3   4   5   6   7
tives of the department and the school.
2. is an effective planner in terms of both short-range   1   2   3   4   5   6   7
and long-range goals and contingencies.
3. projects program changes with the faculty to meet   1   2   3   4   5   6   7
the student needs in learning experiences, materials,
equipment, counseling, facilities, and library ac-
quisitions.
4. is effective in getting additional needed facilities for   1   2   3   4   5   6   7
the department (i.e., research facilities, instructional
areas, etc.).
5. creates a climate in which innovative ideas and plans   1   2   3   4   5   6   7
are invited from teachers, other staff members, and
students.
6. utilizes the faculty in development of goals.   1   2   3   4   5   6   7
7. is effective in maintaining departmental morale.   1   2   3   4   5   6   7
8. effectively guides curriculum development.   1   2   3   4   5   6   7
9. maintains high standards for recruitment and reten-   1   2   3   4   5   6   7
tion of personnel.
10. is effective in creating a climate in which good teach-   1   2   3   4   5   6   7
ing can take place.
11. is receptive to constructive suggestions for change.   1   2   3   4   5   6   7
12. is effective in obtaining funds external to the school   1   2   3   4   5   6   7
for use by the department.

(continued on the next page)

F. Daily Operation	1	2	3	4	5	6	7

Comments

The administrator:

1. provides effective leadership to meet the objectives of the department.	1	2	3	4	5	6	7
2. acts as a facilitator to provide a good instructional program.	1	2	3	4	5	6	7
3. utilizes the democratic process in operating the department in all ways, rather than merely when support is desired.	1	2	3	4	5	6	7
4. maintains good working relationships with all instructors.	1	2	3	4	5	6	7
5. takes decisions made by faculty to students for discussion and feedback.	1	2	3	4	5	6	7
6. reports to his/her superiors progress in improvement of instruction in the department.	1	2	3	4	5	6	7
7. manages office staff effectively.	1	2	3	4	5	6	7
8. maintains good working relationships with the athletic department.	1	2	3	4	5	6	7
9. sees that facilities and equipment of the department are cared for and used according to departmental policy.	1	2	3	4	5	6	7
G. Decision Making Abilities	1	2	3	4	5	6	7

Comments

The administrator:

1. exercises good judgment.	1	2	3	4	5	6	7
2. makes sound and timely decisions.	1	2	3	4	5	6	7
3. is able to make sound, logical decisions under stress.	1	2	3	4	5	6	7
4. gathers pertinent facts before acting.	1	2	3	4	5	6	7
5. obtains faculty approval on important matters before going ahead.	1	2	3	4	5	6	7
6. consults with others on important decisions.	1	2	3	4	5	6	7
7. is able to see problems objectively.	1	2	3	4	5	6	7
8. is willing to make changes.	1	2	3	4	5	6	7
9. bases decisions upon clear, well-thought-out theory rather than trial and error.	1	2	3	4	5	6	7
10. makes fair decisions on promotion and salary.	1	2	3	4	5	6	7
11. makes use of a democratic/participatory approach to leadership.	1	2	3	4	5	6	7
12. makes all policy decisions a matter of group discussions and decision.	1	2	3	4	5	6	7
H. Problem Solving Ability	1	2	3	4	5	6	7

Comments

The administrator:

1. has the ability to identify simple objectives with manageable goals in problem solving.	1	2	3	4	5	6	7
2. is able to anticipate and specify most outcomes of alternative solutions to a problem.	1	2	3	4	5	6	7

(continued on the next page)

3. suggests alternative solutions to problems from which the staff can choose to implement.	1	2	3	4	5	6	7
4. initiates a preferred approach to solving a problem.	1	2	3	4	5	6	7
5. is able to mediate differences among staff effectively.	1	2	3	4	5	6	7
6. is alert to potential problems when plans are not working out.	1	2	3	4	5	6	7
7. approaches problem-solving on a systematic basis.	1	2	3	4	5	6	7
8. is able to select feasible alternatives that seem most consistent with a problem or goal.	1	2	3	4	5	6	7
9. is able to cope with unanticipated events.	1	2	3	4	5	6	7
10. is able to delineate the exact nature of problems and formulate clear goals.	1	2	3	4	5	6	7

Directions for Evaluating
the Physical Education Teacher

NAME _____

This evaluation instrument consists of four major categories that are identified by Roman numerals. Within each major category there are varying numbers of subcategories that are identified by capital letters. *These are the ratings we are interested in.* To the right of each subcategory heading you will find a scale from 1–7. After you have examined the statements listed under each subcategory, circle the number for the subcategory that best represents your opinion of that area. The numerous statements (listed by Arabic numerals) are used merely as an aid to help you make a better evaluation of the subcategory rating. These statements also have the 1–7 scale and, in addition, some may be answered NO or YES (if the response is NO circle 1, if the response is YES circle 7). The individual statements ratings can be "eyeballed" to determine the subcategory rating or the statements rated can be added and divided by the number of items rated (N) to determine an average subcategory rating. There may be statements that *do not apply* to your situation or *demand information not available* to you. If this is true, simply *omit responding* to those items. Add any additional comments in the left-hand margin.

EXAMPLE:

I. The Teacher in the Profession

A. Professional Preparation   1   2   3   4   5 ⑥ 7
Comments
  The teacher:
  1. has a valid teaching certificate.   1   2   3   4   5   6   ⑦
  2. has an undergraduate major or minor in physical   1   2   3   4   5   6   ⑦
     education.
  3. has a background in various classes in methods of   1   2   ③   4   5   6   7
     teaching physical education.

Approximate visually or add numbers
and divide by N for subcategory rating
(i.e., 17 ÷ 3 = 5.7).

Assessment of the Physical Education Teacher

I. The Teacher in the Profession

A. Professional Preparation   1 2 3 4 5 6 7
Comments
The teacher:
1. has a valid teaching certificate.   1 2 3 4 5 6 7
2. has an undergraduate major or minor in physical education.   1 2 3 4 5 6 7
3. has a background in various classes in methods of teaching physical education.   1 2 3 4 5 6 7
4. has had course(s) in individual, dual, and team sports.   1 2 3 4 5 6 7
5. has a current safety and first aid card.   1 2 3 4 5 6 7
6. has taken a course in the care and prevention of injuries.   1 2 3 4 5 6 7
7. has taken courses in the rules and officiating of sports.   1 2 3 4 5 6 7
8. has a background in and a knowledge of a workable intramural program.   1 2 3 4 5 6 7
9. is knowledgeable concerning human movement patterns.   1 2 3 4 5 6 7

B. Educational Implications   1 2 3 4 5 6 7
Comments
The teacher:
1. has an understanding of the role of physical education in the educational program.   1 2 3 4 5 6 7
2. accepts the basic general philosophy of physical education consistent with the role of the school district.   1 2 3 4 5 6 7
3. can explain the aims, significance, and interrelationship of physical education, health, and recreation.   1 2 3 4 5 6 7
4. has participated as a member of the faculty of the school, and assumes professional responsibilities.   1 2 3 4 5 6 7
5. is aware of school and staff discipline policies as they relate to the educational process.   1 2 3 4 5 6 7
6. understands the place of interscholastic competition in the educational program.   1 2 3 4 5 6 7
7. is aware of, and adheres to league, state, and national rules and regulations pertaining to physical education and athletics.   1 2 3 4 5 6 7

C. Ongoing Education   1 2 3 4 5 6 7
Comments:
The teacher:
1. attends clinics, workshops, seminars, and/or classes relating to physical education.   1 2 3 4 5 6 7

241

(continued on the next page)

    2. is an active member of a professional association relating to physical education.   1 2 3 4 5 6 7

    3. subscribes to professional journals relating to physical education.   1 2 3 4 5 6 7

    4. evaluates and uses new materials when appropriate.   1 2 3 4 5 6 7

    5. has knowledge of current trends in curriculum and school planning.   1 2 3 4 5 6 7

  D. Personal Evaluation   1 2 3 4 5 6 7

Comments

    The teacher:

    1. conducts a self-evaluation periodically on teaching ability and expertise.   1 2 3 4 5 6 7

    2. asks others for an evaluation of his/her teaching ability and expertise each year.   1 2 3 4 5 6 7

    3. periodically evaluates the progress of his/her program.   1 2 3 4 5 6 7

    4. keeps the administration informed about the physical education program.   1 2 3 4 5 6 7

II. Instructional Responsibilities

  A. Class Management   1 2 3 4 5 6 7

Comments

    The teacher:

    1. plans the program so that it is consistent with the philosophy of the school.   1 2 3 4 5 6 7

    2. has developed and clearly written program objectives.   1 2 3 4 5 6 7

    3. plans activities on a progression from unit to unit; grade to grade.   1 2 3 4 5 6 7

    4. has a current written course of study for each activity.   1 2 3 4 5 6 7

    5. has a written unit of instruction within each course of study.   1 2 3 4 5 6 7

    6. has written lesson plans made from each unit of instruction.   1 2 3 4 5 6 7

    7. uses student input in planning class activities.   1 2 3 4 5 6 7

    8. utilizes student leadership whenever possible by providing opportunities for teaching, coaching, officiating, and demonstrating.   1 2 3 4 5 6 7

    9. conducts classes in an orderly but informal atmosphere.   1 2 3 4 5 6 7

    10. establishes behavioral expectations consistent with a good learning climate.   1 2 3 4 5 6 7

    11. uses facilities and equipment to the maximum.   1 2 3 4 5 6 7

    12. places a high emphasis on good general health.   1 2 3 4 5 6 7

    13. is open to experiments with innovative ideas.   1 2 3 4 5 6 7

243

(*continued on the next page*)

14. utilizes a variety of evaluation methods. 1 2 3 4 5 6 7
15. has criteria for evaluation that relates directly to the 1 2 3 4 5 6 7
objectives being sought.
B. Instructional Skills 1 2 3 4 5 6 7
Comments
The teacher:
1. emphasizes and demonstrates good fundametal tech- 1 2 3 4 5 6 7
niques and skills in each activity taught.
2. utilizes a variety of teaching methods in presenting 1 2 3 4 5 6 7
instructional materials.
3. can demonstrate or teach another to demonstrate 1 2 3 4 5 6 7
skills and movement essential to instruction.
4. uses audio-visual media in classes when necessary. 1 2 3 4 5 6 7
5. recognizes the need for individual instruction for 1 2 3 4 5 6 7
students.
6. places a high emphasis on carry-over value and life- 1 2 3 4 5 6 7
time fitness for each activity.
7. offers a wide variety of planned activities. 1 2 3 4 5 6 7
8. offers coed and corecreational activities whenever 1 2 3 4 5 6 7
appropriate.
9. secures and holds the attention and interest of the 1 2 3 4 5 6 7
students effectively.
C. Knowledge of Subject Matter 1 2 3 4 5 6 7
Comments
The teacher:
1. knows the techniques required to perform each skill 1 2 3 4 5 6 7
taught.
2. realizes the importance of physical fitness and its re- 1 2 3 4 5 6 7
lationship to the overall health of students.
3. knows appropriate methods of teaching activities. 1 2 3 4 5 6 7
4. knows basic physical growth and development pat- 1 2 3 4 5 6 7
terns of age groups.
5. has a general knowledge of the anatomical structure 1 2 3 4 5 6 7
of the body.
6. can analyze the mechanics of movement and 1 2 3 4 5 6 7
evaluate efficiency in movement.
7. is knowledgeable in regard to purchase, care, use, 1 2 3 4 5 6 7
and storage of equipment and supplies.
8. is knowledgeable concerning sports injuries. 1 2 3 4 5 6 7
D. Discipline 1 2 3 4 5 6 7
Comments
The teacher:
1. maintains self-control and emotional stability under 1 2 3 4 5 6 7
stress.
2. conducts classes in an orderly manner. 1 2 3 4 5 6 7
3. has the respect of students. 1 2 3 4 5 6 7
4. informs students of classroom standards. 1 2 3 4 5 6 7

245

(*continued on the next page*)

5. holds a line between student and teacher so the student is aware that the teacher *is* the teacher.	1	2	3	4	5	6	7
6. has rules that are reasonable and prudent.	1	2	3	4	5	6	7
7. is consistent in dealings with the class.	1	2	3	4	5	6	7
E. Attendance	1	2	3	4	5	6	7

Comments

The teacher:

1. follows the school policies on class attendance.	1	2	3	4	5	6	7
2. informs students of attendance policies.	1	2	3	4	5	6	7
3. keeps accurate, up-to-date attendance records.	1	2	3	4	5	6	7
4. has a good method of readmitting ill or injured students.	1	2	3	4	5	6	7
5. has made provisions for make-up work.							

III. Personal Qualities

A. Human Relations	1	2	3	4	5	6	7

Comments

The teacher:

1. is flexible in attitude towards youth and societal changes.	1	2	3	4	5	6	7
2. recognizes and respects individual differences in students.	1	2	3	4	5	6	7
3. motivates students to learn.	1	2	3	4	5	6	7
4. projects an enthusiastic and dynamic attitude in dealing with people.	1	2	3	4	5	6	7
5. maintains an open, positive working relationship with students.	1	2	3	4	5	6	7
6. is objective in praising.	1	2	3	4	5	6	7
7. is objective in criticizing.	1	2	3	4	5	6	7
8. helps create and maintain high morals.	1	2	3	4	5	6	7
9. is honest in relationships with others.	1	2	3	4	5	6	7
B. Personality Traits	1	2	3	4	5	6	7

Comments

The teacher:

1. maintains emotional stability and poise.	1	2	3	4	5	6	7
2. uses appropriate vocabulary, grammar, etc.	1	2	3	4	5	6	7
3. is worthy of emulation of students and colleagues.	1	2	3	4	5	6	7
4. can accept criticism.	1	2	3	4	5	6	7
5. has self-confidence.	1	2	3	4	5	6	7
6. avoids the use of destructive criticism, sarcasm, and ridicule with students.	1	2	3	4	5	6	7
7. has an appropriate sense of humor.	1	2	3	4	5	6	7
8. has the desire to be successful.	1	2	3	4	5	6	7
9. has the ability to admit weaknesses and/or mistakes.	1	2	3	4	5	6	7
10. behaves in a consistent manner.	1	2	3	4	5	6	7
11. possesses high standards and ideals of work.	1	2	3	4	5	6	7

247

(continued on the next page)

12. cooperates with administrators. 　　　　　　　　1 2 3 4 5 6 7
13. has the refinement, character, and objectivity expected of a professional person. 　　　　　1 2 3 4 5 6 7

C. Physical Characteristics 　　　　　　　　　　　1 2 3 4 5 6 7
Comments

The teacher:
1. dresses appropriately. 　　　　　　　　　　　1 2 3 4 5 6 7
2. maintains adequate physical fitness. 　　　　　1 2 3 4 5 6 7
3. possesses adequate skills in the sports he/she teaches. 　　　　　　　　　　　　　　　　1 2 3 4 5 6 7
4. exhibits substantial freedom from annoying or distracting personal mannerisms. 　　　　1 2 3 4 5 6 7

IV. Public Relations

A. Communication Skills 　　　　　　　　　　　　1 2 3 4 5 6 7
Comments

The teacher:
1. is articulate. 　　　　　　　　　　　　　　　1 2 3 4 5 6 7
2. has good command of the English language. 　　1 2 3 4 5 6 7
3. has good writing skills. 　　　　　　　　　　　1 2 3 4 5 6 7
4. uses good grammar. 　　　　　　　　　　　　1 2 3 4 5 6 7
5. can explain aims, significance, and interrelationships of physical education, recreation, and health as a means of furthering public understanding of these fields. 　　　　　　　　　　　　　　　1 2 3 4 5 6 7
6. interprets system-wide policies and develops supplementary physical education policies for students, parents, school personnel, and community. 　1 2 3 4 5 6 7

B. Effective Interpersonal Relationships 　　　　　1 2 3 4 5 6 7
Comments

The teacher:
1. has good rapport with the principal. 　　　　　1 2 3 4 5 6 7
2. has good rapport with the coaching staff and other faculty members. 　　　　　　　　　　1 2 3 4 5 6 7
3. has good rapport with members of the physical education staff. 　　　　　　　　　　　　1 2 3 4 5 6 7
4. has good rapport with parents of students. 　　1 2 3 4 5 6 7
5. has good rapport with students. 　　　　　　　1 2 3 4 5 6 7
6. has good rapport with community groups and organizations. 　　　　　　　　　　　　　　1 2 3 4 5 6 7
7. relates effectively with all socioeconomic, racial, and ethnic groups. 　　　　　　　　　　1 2 3 4 5 6 7

Directions for Evaluating the Physical Education Program

This evaluation instrument consists of six major categories that are identified by Roman numerals. Within each major category there are varying numbers of subcategories that are identified by capital letters. *These are the ratings we are interested in.* To the right of each subcategory heading you will find a scale from 1–7. After you have examined the statements listed under each subcategory, circle the number for the subcategory that best represents your opinion of that area. The numerous statements (listed by Arabic numerals) are used merely as an aid to help you make a better evaluation of the subcategory rating. These statements also have the 1–7 scale and, in addition, some may be answered NO or YES (if the response is NO circle 1, if the response is YES circle 7). The individual statements ratings can be "eyeballed" to determine the subcategory rating or the statements rated can be added and divided by the number of items rated (N) to determine an average subcategory rating. There may be statements that *do not apply* to your situation or *demand information not available* to you. If this is true simply *omit responding* to those items. Add any additional comments in the left-hand margin.

EXAMPLE:

II. Fiscal Management of the Physical Education Program

A. Budget   1 2 ③ 4 5 6 7
Comments

1. The policies governing the expenditure of district   1 2 ③ 4 5 6 7
funds for the physical education program are clearly
stated in written form.

2. The district budget policies are followed in the pro-   1 ② 3 4 5 6 7
gram.

3. The physical education program receives an equit-   1 2 3 ④ 5 6 7
able distribution of funds when compared with
other programs of the educational process.

Approximate visually or add numbers
and divide by N for subcategory rating
(i.e., 9 ÷ 3 = 3).

Assessment of the Physical Education Program

I. Relationship of the Physical Education Program to the Total Educational Program

A. Purposes and Objectives of the Physical Education Program   1 2 3 4 5 6 7

Comments

1. The administration of the school has a clearly written statement of goals and objectives for the physical education program.   1 2 3 4 5 6 7

2. There exists in writing a statement of the philosophy upon which the physical education program is based.   1 2 3 4 5 6 7

3. The physical education program is regarded as an integral part of the educational system of the district.   1 2 3 4 5 6 7

4. Present and future needs of students are considered in planning the desired outcomes of the physical education program.   1 2 3 4 5 6 7

5. The development of the statement of goals and objectives was a combined effort of: 1 2 3 4 5 6 7
   a. physical education personnel.   1 2 3 4 5 6 7
   b. administration.   1 2 3 4 5 6 7
   c. students.   1 2 3 4 5 6 7
   d. the community.

6. The statement of goals and objectives is effectively made known to: 1 2 3 4 5 6 7
   a. physical education personnel.   1 2 3 4 5 6 7
   b. administration.   1 2 3 4 5 6 7
   c. faculty.   1 2 3 4 5 6 7
   d. students.   1 2 3 4 5 6 7
   e. the community.   1 2 3 4 5 6 7

7. All goals and objectives of the statement can be evaluated.   1 2 3 4 5 6 7

8. The physical education program is conducted in accordance with the statement of goals and objectives.   1 2 3 4 5 6 7

9. There is sufficient flexibility and opportunity for the ongoing revision of the statement of goals and objectives as changing conditions warrant by: 1 2 3 4 5 6 7
   a. physical education personnel.   1 2 3 4 5 6 7
   b. administration.   1 2 3 4 5 6 7
   c. students.   1 2 3 4 5 6 7
   d. the community.   1 2 3 4 5 6 7

10. Individual physical education personnel have written statements of goals and objectives for their respective programs.   1 2 3 4 5 6 7

253

(continued on the next page)

11. All goals and objectives are primarily concerned with the welfare of the student.   1 2 3 4 5 6 7

12. All goals and objectives are based on educational objectives.   1 2 3 4 5 6 7

13. The physical education program operates within the framework of the district policy.   1 2 3 4 5 6 7

14. The physical education program is subject to the same administrative control as the total educational program.   1 2 3 4 5 6 7

II. Fiscal Management of the Physical Education Program

A. Budget   1 2 3 4 5 6 7
Comments

1. The policies governing the expenditure of district funds for the physical education program are clearly stated in written form.   1 2 3 4 5 6 7

2. The district budget policies are followed in the program.   1 2 3 4 5 6 7

3. The physical education program receives an equitable distribution of funds when compared with other programs of the educational process.   1 2 3 4 5 6 7

4. The physical education staff prepares a clear, itemized, written annual budget.   1 2 3 4 5 6 7

5. The physical education program stays within its allotted budget.   1 2 3 4 5 6 7

6. Complete financial budgets and records of past years are kept to provide information for evaluation and planning.   1 2 3 4 5 6 7

7. The physical education staff works with the administration in preparing the total budget.   1 2 3 4 5 6 7

8. All members of the physical education program receive a copy of the total school budget and the program budget.   1 2 3 4 5 6 7

9. The physical education program is able to operate efficiently on the allotted budget.   1 2 3 4 5 6 7

B. Equipment and Facilities (Refer to instrument on facilities)   1 2 3 4 5 6 7
Comments

1. There are clearly written policies and procedures regarding the purchase of supplies and equipment.   1 2 3 4 5 6 7

2. All physical education personnel follow the set policies and procedures for purchase of supplies and equipment.   1 2 3 4 5 6 7

3. Equipment in the program is sufficient.   1 2 3 4 5 6 7

4. All personnel have input into determining the type and quality of equipment needed.   1 2 3 4 5 6 7

255

(*continued on the next page*)

5. Supplies in the program are sufficient.   1   2   3   4   5   6   7

6. All personnel have input into determining the type and quality of supplies needed.   1   2   3   4   5   6   7

7. The safety and comfort of the student is the primary consideration in the choosing of equipment.   1   2   3   4   5   6   7

8. The equipment is periodically checked to insure the safety of the participant.   1   2   3   4   5   6   7

9. Provision is made for the student who cannot afford physical education clothing or equipment.   1   2   3   4   5   6   7

10. An up-to-date inventory is kept on all equipment and supplies.   1   2   3   4   5   6   7

11. Equipment is properly cared for.   1   2   3   4   5   6   7

12. There are adequate storage facilities for all equipment.   1   2   3   4   5   6   7

13. There is an effective set procedure for issue and return of equipment and supplies.   1   2   3   4   5   6   7

14. Someone is designated the responsibility for the care and issue of equipment.   1   2   3   4   5   6   7

15. Adequate, secured individual lockers are available to all students in physical education.   1   2   3   4   5   6   7

16. All instructors are required to take inventory of the equipment and supplies used in their teaching at the end of each unit.   1   2   3   4   5   6   7

17. All damaged equipment is kept from use until properly repaired.   1   2   3   4   5   6   7

18. Satisfactory arrangements are made for the repair and reconditioning of equipment.   1   2   3   4   5   6   7

19. Long-range planning is effective in replacing and purchasing major equipment items.   1   2   3   4   5   6   7

20. The advantages of early buying are clearly understood by personnel.   1   2   3   4   5   6   7

21. An effective method of marking equipment and supplies is used.   1   2   3   4   5   6   7

22. The best equipment and supplies are obtained within the limits of the budget.   1   2   3   4   5   6   7

23. There are adequate facilities, indoors and outdoors, for the program.   1   2   3   4   5   6   7

III. Relationship of the Physical Education Program to the Community

A. Public Relations   1   2   3   4   5   6   7
Comments

1. There is cooperative effort by all instructors in the program to promote good relations with the total community (news media, parents, students, etc.).   1   2   3   4   5   6   7

2. The department has obtained facts about what the public knows and believes about educational values and needs.   1   2   3   4   5   6   7

(continued on the next page)

    3. Teacher-pupil planning techniques are used.   1   2   3   4   5   6   7

    4. The community is informed and allowed input before any major changes are made in the physical education program.   1   2   3   4   5   6   7

    5. The community is informed in writing of the physical education program objectives and policies.   1   2   3   4   5   6   7

    6. All instructors understand the importance and principles of good public relations.   1   2   3   4   5   6   7

    7. The entire school faculty is kept informed of what is happening in the physical education department.   1   2   3   4   5   6   7

    8. Physical education instructors are involved with and support other areas of the educational system.   1   2   3   4   5   6   7

    9. The physical education department uses demonstrations to effectively interpret the school program to the public.   1   2   3   4   5   6   7

    10. The physical education department prepares and distributes handbooks and information bulletins.   1   2   3   4   5   6   7

    11. The physical education teacher recognizes the value of tact, courtesy, and friendliness toward those he comes in contact with.   1   2   3   4   5   6   7

    12. There is a written and implemented plan to acquaint the community, students, and faculty with the different aspects of the physical education program.   1   2   3   4   5   6   7

  B. Community   1   2   3   4   5   6   7
Comments

    1. Members of the community are made aware of the goals and objectives of the program.   1   2   3   4   5   6   7

    2. The physical education program meets the needs and interests of the community.   1   2   3   4   5   6   7

    3. The community supports all areas of the physical education program.   1   2   3   4   5   6   7

    4. All school physical education facilities are made available to the community whenever they are not in use for school activities.   1   2   3   4   5   6   7

    5. Channels are provided for community input into the program.   1   2   3   4   5   6   7

    6. Written policies are available regarding the use of school (physical education) facilities.   1   2   3   4   5   6   7

IV. Administration of the Physical Education Program

  A. Organization and Planning   1   2   3   4   5   6   7
Comments

    1. The physical education program has written goals and objectives that are adopted by the school administration.   1   2   3   4   5   6   7

    2. All policies and procedures are based upon the welfare of the physical education student.   1   2   3   4   5   6   7

(*continued on the next page*)

3. The physical education program for both boys and girls, including athletics and intramurals, is under one department.   1 2 3 4 5 6 7

4. All students are required to take physical education according to state requirements.   1 2 3 4 5 6 7

5. The physical education department has regularly scheduled meetings to develop policy, solve problems, and design programs.   1 2 3 4 5 6 7

6. There are clearly written policies and job descriptions concerning selection of personnel.   1 2 3 4 5 6 7

7. There are clearly written policies concerning retention of staff.   1 2 3 4 5 6 7

8. Suggestions, problems, and program changes are easily made to the school administration.   1 2 3 4 5 6 7

9. Classes are organized based on the abilities and needs of the physical education student.   1 2 3 4 5 6 7

10. Teacher-student ratio is adequate for effective teaching.   1 2 3 4 5 6 7

11. The physical education program requires physical examinations for participation.   1 2 3 4 5 6 7

12. There is a written, set, procedure to be followed in case of accidents.   1 2 3 4 5 6 7

13. Protective equipment is provided according to the demands of the activity.   1 2 3 4 5 6 7

14. The physical education staff cooperatively plans and conducts coeducational instruction and activities.   1 2 3 4 5 6 7

15. All district physical education staff plan together to provide a total physical education program for the district.   1 2 3 4 5 6 7

16. There is a defined, written process to evaluate the effectiveness of policies and procedures of the physical education program.   1 2 3 4 5 6 7

17. Evaluation of the physical education staff is done yearly by the: 1 2 3 4 5 6 7
    a. administration.   1 2 3 4 5 6 7
    b. students.   1 2 3 4 5 6 7
    c. community.   1 2 3 4 5 6 7
    d. self-evaluation.   1 2 3 4 5 6 7

18. Evaluation of the program is done on a regular basis by the: 1 2 3 4 5 6 7
    a. administration.   1 2 3 4 5 6 7
    b. students.   1 2 3 4 5 6 7
    c. community.   1 2 3 4 5 6 7
    d. physical education staff.   1 2 3 4 5 6 7

19. In-service education is provided for the physical education staff.   1 2 3 4 5 6 7

20. Written duties of all program coordinators are available.   1 2 3 4 5 6 7

261

(continued on the next page)

21. There are written departmental policies and proce-   1 2 3 4 5 6 7
dures for:
   a. issue of lockers/baskets.   1 2 3 4 5 6 7
   b. issue of towels.   1 2 3 4 5 6 7
   c. issue of locks.   1 2 3 4 5 6 7
   d. uniforms.   1 2 3 4 5 6 7
   e. required showers.   1 2 3 4 5 6 7
   f. attendance and absences.   1 2 3 4 5 6 7
   g. transportation.   1 2 3 4 5 6 7

B. Personnel (refer to instrument on the Physical Educator)   1 2 3 4 5 6 7

Comments

1. All physical education staff meet state certification.   1 2 3 4 5 6 7
2. All physical education staff have a major or minor   1 2 3 4 5 6 7
degree in physical education.
3. All staff are selected who have values that are in ac-   1 2 3 4 5 6 7
cordance with community standards.
4. Nonteaching personnel comply with the state regu-   1 2 3 4 5 6 7
lations for such people.
5. All staff members effectively perform all functions   1 2 3 4 5 6 7
as faculty members.
6. All staff members carry the equivalent workload as   1 2 3 4 5 6 7
other faculty.
7. All staff are active members in their professional or-   1 2 3 4 5 6 7
ganizations.
8. All staff keep informed of current developments in   1 2 3 4 5 6 7
the professional field.
9. All staff maintain an active interest in professional   1 2 3 4 5 6 7
advancement.
10. All staff members show professionalism through at-   1 2 3 4 5 6 7
tendance at in-service programs.

C. Evaluation   1 2 3 4 5 6 7

Comments

1. The physical education program is effectively and   1 2 3 4 5 6 7
unbiasedly evaluated yearly by the administration.
2. Instructors are evaluated annually using an assess-   1 2 3 4 5 6 7
ment instrument.
3. The physical education department chairperson   1 2 3 4 5 6 7
makes a comprehensive written evaluation of the
program annually.
4. All physical education instructors have the oppor-   1 2 3 4 5 6 7
tunity to evaluate the total physical education pro-
gram.
5. There is an effective method for students to evalu-   1 2 3 4 5 6 7
ate the program annually.
6. There is an effective method for members of the   1 2 3 4 5 6 7
community to evaluate the program annually.

(*continued on the next page*)

7. There is an effective method of evaluating whether the goals and objectives of the program are being met.   1   2   3   4   5   6   7

8. The physical education program is considered valuable by the: 1   2   3   4   5   6   7
    a. students.   1   2   3   4   5   6   7
    b. community.   1   2   3   4   5   6   7
    c. administration.   1   2   3   4   5   6   7

V. The Curriculum in the Physical Education Program

A. Course of Study   1   2   3   4   5   6   7
Comments

1. The course of study is written out and is up-to-date.   1   2   3   4   5   6   7
2. The course of study is available upon request.   1   2   3   4   5   6   7
3. The instructional program is designed to facilitate the transition from elementary to high school level.   1   2   3   4   5   6   7
4. The curriculum meets or exceeds state requirements for physical education.   1   2   3   4   5   6   7
5. Progression in learning skills is provided.   1   2   3   4   5   6   7
6. The curriculum is flexible and allows for individual differences.   1   2   3   4   5   6   7
7. Instructional activities are well planned and organized throughout the district.   1   2   3   4   5   6   7
8. Planning considerations include the students: 1   2   3   4   5   6   7
    a. needs.   1   2   3   4   5   6   7
    b. interests.   1   2   3   4   5   6   7
    c. former experiences.   1   2   3   4   5   6   7
9. Data from health appraisals are utilized to make instruction more effective.   1   2   3   4   5   6   7
10. Experiences in leisure-time activities are included.   1   2   3   4   5   6   7
11. Adaptive physical education is part of the regular program.   1   2   3   4   5   6   7
12. Activities for students who may have special physical education needs are provided.   1   2   3   4   5   6   7
13. Elective programs geared to individual student interests are included.   1   2   3   4   5   6   7
14. Coeducational instruction is provided in: 1   2   3   4   5   6   7
    a. individual sports.   1   2   3   4   5   6   7
    b. dual sports.   1   2   3   4   5   6   7
    c. team sports.   1   2   3   4   5   6   7
15. The curriculum is well balanced.   1   2   3   4   5   6   7
16. A wide variety of activities is offered to provide experiences in many skills.   1   2   3   4   5   6   7
17. Students have an opportunity for input in selection of activities.   1   2   3   4   5   6   7

265

(continued on the next page)

18. Students have an opportunity for input into the organization of the program.	1	2	3	4	5	6	7
19. Conditioning and total fitness activities are offered in the curriculum.	1	2	3	4	5	6	7
20. Aquatic activities (water safety) are provided for.	1	2	3	4	5	6	7
21. Outdoor educational activities are included.	1	2	3	4	5	6	7
22. Interscholastic athletic programs are provided for the more skilled students.	1	2	3	4	5	6	7
23. Intramural programs are provided for:	1	2	3	4	5	6	7
a. boys.	1	2	3	4	5	6	7
b. girls.	1	2	3	4	5	6	7
c. boys and girls competing together.	1	2	3	4	5	6	7
24. There is a written plan for annual evaluation of the curriculum.	1	2	3	4	5	6	7
25. Physical education is considered part of the total school curriculum.	1	2	3	4	5	6	7
26. Students have the opportunity to evaluate the curriculum.	1	2	3	4	5	6	7
27. Other areas of curriculum (band, athletics, etc.) cannot be substituted for physical education.	1	2	3	4	5	6	7
28. Set, written procedures are used in placing students in the adaptive physical education program.	1	2	3	4	5	6	7
29. Opportunities are provided in the curriculum that develop:	1	2	3	4	5	6	7
a. strength.	1	2	3	4	5	6	7
b. skills.	1	2	3	4	5	6	7
c. cardiovascular fitness.	1	2	3	4	5	6	7
30. The curriculum provides opportunities for psychological development in:	1	2	3	4	5	6	7
a. activities that are based on psychological needs of the age groups (coeducational).	1	2	3	4	5	6	7
b. activities that provide emotional outlets for students.	1	2	3	4	5	6	7
c. use of natural play activities.	1	2	3	4	5	6	7
d. the development of positive self-concept through success in activities.	1	2	3	4	5	6	7
e. interest of the group in specific activities.	1	2	3	4	5	6	7
f. challenging, yet achievable activities.	1	2	3	4	5	6	7
g. sufficient time in each activity to learn.	1	2	3	4	5	6	7
h. creativity.	1	2	3	4	5	6	7
31. The curriculum provides opportunity for sociological development in:	1	2	3	4	5	6	7
a. leisure-time activities.	1	2	3	4	5	6	7
b. team play.	1	2	3	4	5	6	7
c. individual play.	1	2	3	4	5	6	7
d. leadership.	1	2	3	4	5	6	7
32. The curriculum is based on community needs and facilities.	1	2	3	4	5	6	7

267

(*continued on the next page*)

ADDITIONAL CURRICULA FOR COLLEGES

33. Courses are provided in the following areas:

	1	2	3	4	5	6	7
a. anatomy.	1	2	3	4	5	6	7
b. physiology.	1	2	3	4	5	6	7
c. kinesiology.	1	2	3	4	5	6	7
d. physiology of exercise.	1	2	3	4	5	6	7
e. human movement.	1	2	3	4	5	6	7
f. teaching methods.	1	2	3	4	5	6	7
g. principles.	1	2	3	4	5	6	7
h. evaluation.	1	2	3	4	5	6	7
i. skill courses (including strategies and rules).	1	2	3	4	5	6	7
j. psychology of sport.	1	2	3	4	5	6	7
k. sociology of sport.	1	2	3	4	5	6	7
l. facilities/equipment.	1	2	3	4	5	6	7
m. motor learning.	1	2	3	4	5	6	7
n. behavioral objectives.	1	2	3	4	5	6	7
o. first aid.	1	2	3	4	5	6	7
p. adaptive.	1	2	3	4	5	6	7
q. organization/planning.	1	2	3	4	5	6	7
r. curriculum.	1	2	3	4	5	6	7
s. growth and development.	1	2	3	4	5	6	7
t. history.	1	2	3	4	5	6	7
u. philosophy.	1	2	3	4	5	6	7

Directions for Evaluating the Intramural Program

This evaluation instrument consists of six major categories that are identified by Roman numerals. Within each major category there are varying numbers of subcategories that are identified by capital letters. *These are the ratings we are interested in.* To the right of each subcategory heading you will find a scale from 1–7. After you have examined the statements listed under each subcategory, circle the number for the subcategory that best represents your opinion of that area. The numerous statements (listed by Arabic numerals) are used merely as an aid to help you make a better evaluation of the subcategory rating. These statements also have the 1–7 scale and, in addition, some may be answered NO or YES (if the response is NO circle 1, if the response is YES circle 7). The individual statements rating can be "eyeballed" to determine the subcategory rating or the statements rated can be added and divided by the number of items rated (N) to determine an average subcategory rating. There may be statements that *do not apply* to your situation or *demand information not available* to you. If this is true, simply *omit responding* to those items. Add any additional comments in the left-hand margin.

EXAMPLE:

II. Fiscal Management	
A. Revenue/Income	1 2 3 ④ 5 6 7
Comments	
1. Policies governing the revenue and expenditure of funds are clearly stated in written form.	1 2 3 4 5 6 ⑦
2. Policies are known and clearly understood by all people involved in the program.	1 2 3 ④ 5 6 7
3. Consideration is given to the equitable distribution of funds to all sports in the program.	① 2 3 4 5 6 7
	Approximate visually or add numbers and divide by N for subcategory rating (i.e., 12 ÷ 3 = 4).

Assessment of the Intramural Program

I. Relationship of the Intramural Program to the Total Educational Program

    A. Purposes and Objectives of the Intramural Program   1 2 3 4 5 6 7
Comments
       1. The administration of the school has a clearly writ-   1 2 3 4 5 6 7
          ten statement of goals and objectives of the intra-
          mural program.
       2. The statement of goals and objectives was developed   1 2 3 4 5 6 7
          and designed for this particular school's intramural
          program.
       3. The intramural staff, administration, and student   1 2 3 4 5 6 7
          body were involved in the development of the   1 2 3 4 5 6 7
          statement of goals and objectives.
       4. Efforts have been made to acquaint the student   1 2 3 4 5 6 7
          body with the statement of goals and objectives.
       5. The goals and objectives are specifically stated in   1 2 3 4 5 6 7
          terms that allow them to be evaluated.
       6. There are sufficient flexibility and opportunity for   1 2 3 4 5 6 7
          the ongoing revision of the statement as chang-
          ing conditions warrant it.
       7. The goals and objectives are educationally sound.   1 2 3 4 5 6 7
       8. The intramural program is an extension of the phys-   1 2 3 4 5 6 7
          ical education program.

II. Fiscal Management

    A. Revenue/Income   1 2 3 4 5 6 7
Comments
       1. Policies governing the revenue and expenditure of   1 2 3 4 5 6 7
          funds for intramurals are clearly stated in written
          form.
       2. The policies are known and clearly understood by   1 2 3 4 5 6 7
          all people involved in the program.
       3. Consideration is given to the equitable distribution   1 2 3 4 5 6 7
          of funds to all sports in the program.
       4. All income generated by the intramural program   1 2 3 4 5 6 7
          goes into a general intramural fund for the conduct
          of the total program.
       5. All fund-raising projects are approved and coordi-   1 2 3 4 5 6 7
          nated by the intramural director.
       6. Provisions are made for an annual audit.   1 2 3 4 5 6 7
    B. Budget   1 2 3 4 5 6 7
Comments
       1. The intramural director prepares a clear, itemized,   1 2 3 4 5 6 7
          written intramural budget.

273

(continued on the next page)

2. The administration is informed about all aspects of the intramural budget.   1 2 3 4 5 6 7

3. Students are effectively utilized in formulating the intramural budget.   1 2 3 4 5 6 7

4. Adequate financial records are kept by the intramural director (or a bookkeeper) during the year to facilitate the proper use of the budget.   1 2 3 4 5 6 7

5. Good financial records for past years are maintained to provide information for evaluation and future planning.   1 2 3 4 5 6 7   1 2 3 4 5 6 7

6. The program operates as efficiently as it can on the allotted budget.   1 2 3 4 5 6 7

7. The program stays within its allotted budget.   1 2 3 4 5 6 7

8. The intramural director is accountable for use of all funds allotted in the budget.   1 2 3 4 5 6 7

9. The budget is completely supported by school funds.   1 2 3 4 5 6 7

C. Equipment   1 2 3 4 5 6 7
Comments

1. There is a clearly written policy regarding the purchase of intramural supplies and equipment.   1 2 3 4 5 6 7

2. Adequate equipment and supplies are provided for participants in each sport.   1 2 3 4 5 6 7

3. Effective long-range planning is done to provide for replacement and purchase of major equipment items.   1 2 3 4 5 6 7

4. Adequate storage is provided for equipment and supplies.   1 2 3 4 5 6 7

5. Adequate arrangements are made for the repair and reconditioning of equipment.   1 2 3 4 5 6 7

6. There is an effective set procedure for issue and return of equipment and supplies.   1 2 3 4 5 6 7

7. All intramural personnel assist in enforcing rules concerning the use of equipment and supplies.   1 2 3 4 5 6 7

8. An inventory is taken at the end of each sport season of the equipment and supplies used in that sport season.   1 2 3 4 5 6 7

9. Damaged equipment is kept from use until adequately repaired.   1 2 3 4 5 6 7

10. An effective method of marking equipment and supplies is used.   1 2 3 4 5 6 7

11. The best equipment and supplies are obtained within the limits of the budget.   1 2 3 4 5 6 7

D. Officials   1 2 3 4 5 6 7
Comments

1. There is a clearly written policy regarding how a coach or team files a grievance with the intramural council.   1 2 3 4 5 6 7

(*continued on the next page*)

2. There is a designated person responsible for assigning all officials for intramural contests.   1 2 3 4 5 6 7

3. There is a designated person responsible for paying or keeping hours of all officials at intramural contests.   1 2 3 4 5 6 7

4. Properly qualified officials are obtained for all contests.   1 2 3 4 5 6 7

5. Adequate security is provided for officials during and after intramural contests.   1 2 3 4 5 6 7

6. There is an effective system established for training officials.   1 2 3 4 5 6 7

III. Relationship of the Intramural Program to the Community

A. Public Relations   1 2 3 4 5 6 7
Comments

1. Dates and times of all intramural contests are publicized in the school paper, bulletins, PA systems, etc.   1 2 3 4 5 6 7

2. There is a person responsible for reporting the results of each intramural contest to the school and/or local newspaper.   1 2 3 4 5 6 7

3. There is a publicity chairperson for intramurals.   1 2 3 4 5 6 7

4. Members of the community (student body, parents) are informed in writing of intramural policies.   1 2 3 4 5 6 7

5. Past procedures for publicity are kept on file for reference.   1 2 3 4 5 6 7

IV. Administration of the Intramural Program

A. Organization and Planning   1 2 3 4 5 6 7
Comments

1. The procedures for reaching the goals and objectives of the intramural program are thoroughly and clearly identified.   1 2 3 4 5 6 7

2. The intramural director helps in coordinating the scheduling of school events in order to obtain maximum utilization of existing facilities.   1 2 3 4 5 6 7

3. All facilities are made available to both boys and girls on an equitable basis if the intramural programs are separate.   1 2 3 4 5 6 7

4. An adequate insurance program is provided for students.   1 2 3 4 5 6 7

5. There is an established intramural council composed of faculty, students, and the intramural director.   1 2 3 4 5 6 7

277

(*continued on the next page*)

6. The intramural council has regularly scheduled meetings to develop policy and resolve problems.   1   2   3   4   5   6   7

7. Faculty and students are responsible for the planning of the intramural program content.   1   2   3   4   5   6   7

8. Intramural policies are developed with input from both faculty and students.   1   2   3   4   5   6   7

9. The implementation of intramural policies is done by the students with advice from the intramural director.   1   2   3   4   5   6   7

10. Grievance procedures are clearly written and made known to all participants.   1   2   3   4   5   6   7

B. Rules and Regulations   1   2   3   4   5   6   7
Comments

1. All students receive a copy of the rules governing intramurals.   1   2   3   4   5   6   7

2. All coaches provide their athletes a written statement of rules and regulations relative to their individual sport.   1   2   3   4   5   6   7

C. Legal Aspects   1   2   3   4   5   6   7
Comments

1. All legal aspects related to intramurals are considered.   1   2   3   4   5   6   7

    a. negligence.   1   2   3   4   5   6   7

    b. facilities.   1   2   3   4   5   6   7

    c. insurance.   1   2   3   4   5   6   7

    d. personal exchanges.

D. Intramural Program Curriculum   1   2   3   4   5   6   7
Comments

1. There is a broad range of sports available for all students.   1   2   3   4   5   6   7

2. The educational value of sports is foremost in the intramural philosophy.   1   2   3   4   5   6   7

3. All interested students have an opportunity to participate in some phase of the program.   1   2   3   4   5   6   7

4. Established intramural sports seasons permit the participant maximum conditioning and development (i.e., adequate practice time is permitted before the competitive season begins and there is adequate time between contests for improvement of performance).   1   2   3   4   5   6   7

5. Scheduling of contests is established so that overlap of sport seasons is prevented.   1   2   3   4   5   6   7

6. The activities included in the intramural program are outgrowths of the physical education instructional program.   1   2   3   4   5   6   7

279

(continued on the next page)

E. Personnel   1 2 3 4 5 6 7
Comments
1. An adequate staff is provided to run the program effectively.   1 2 3 4 5 6 7
2. Student help is encouraged and utilized.   1 2 3 4 5 6 7
3. All student position responsibilities are defined.   1 2 3 4 5 6 7
4. All staff responsibilities are defined.   1 2 3 4 5 6 7
5. All student responsibility positions are evaluated yearly by the intramural director.   1 2 3 4 5 6 7
6. All staff are evaluated yearly by the intramural director.   1 2 3 4 5 6 7

F. Evaluation Procedures   1 2 3 4 5 6 7
Comments
1. All aspects of the intramural program are evaluated in terms of the contribution it makes toward the fulfillment of goals and objectives.   1 2 3 4 5 6 7
2. Evaluation of the total intramural program is completed by personnel within the program, students, and staff, each year and filed with the intramural director.   1 2 3 4 5 6 7
3. Evaluation of each individual sports program is done by the sports managers of that particular program and filed with the intramural director.   1 2 3 4 5 6 7
4. Information derived from these evaluations is used when considering program or policy changes.   1 2 3 4 5 6 7

V. Facilities for the Intramural Program

A. Facilities   1 2 3 4 5 6 7
Comments
1. The intramural facilities are constantly being reevaluated to determine present effectiveness and future needs.   1 2 3 4 5 6 7
2. Goals have been established to anticipate future needs, foster orderly growth, and provide renovation of existing facilities.   1 2 3 4 5 6 7
3. Community facilities are utilized whenever necessary to avoid duplication and to make use of superior facilities.   1 2 3 4 5 6 7
4. There is adequate space and/or areas for indoor programs.   1 2 3 4 5 6 7
5. There is adequate space and/or areas for outdoor sports.   1 2 3 4 5 6 7
6. There is an adequate training room and/or first aid station to provide services for participants.   1 2 3 4 5 6 7
7. There is adequate scoreboard equipment available.   1 2 3 4 5 6 7

(*continued on the next page*)

8. Adequate space is available for the proper storage of intramural equipment and materials.   1 2 3 4 5 6 7

9. There are sufficient lockers available to meet the demands of the athletic, physical education, and intramural programs.   1 2 3 4 5 6 7

10. There are proper shower and drying room facilities available.   1 2 3 4 5 6 7

VI. Student in the Intramural Program

A. Participation (i.e., meeting needs of students)   1 2 3 4 5 6 7
Comments

1. All students are given equitable opportunity to participate in intramural sports.   1 2 3 4 5 6 7

2. The intramural program is designed to offer a wide variety of opportunities to meet the individual differences of the student body.   1 2 3 4 5 6 7

3. Regular channels of communication are established to impart program values and standards to all students.   1 2 3 4 5 6 7

4. All participants are protected from a loss of class time by proper scheduling of intramural events.   1 2 3 4 5 6 7

5. Students are encouraged to participate in a variety of sports.   1 2 3 4 5 6 7

6. Students are permitted to participate in only one sport at a time.   1 2 3 4 5 6 7

7. There are general information announcements and meetings for new students regarding the intramural program.   1 2 3 4 5 6 7

B. Health Considerations   1 2 3 4 5 6 7
Comments

1. All students are required to have an accident insurance policy before being allowed to participate.   1 2 3 4 5 6 7

2. All students are required to take a physical examination before playing on an intramural team.   1 2 3 4 5 6 7

3. All facilities meet fire and safety code requirements.   1 2 3 4 5 6 7

4. There is adequate lighting to meet minimum requirements in all facilities.   1 2 3 4 5 6 7

5. The playing floors and fields are properly marked and finished to provide maximum safety.   1 2 3 4 5 6 7

6. Arrangements are made to have medical service available during intramural activities.   1 2 3 4 5 6 7

7. A clearly written policy is made known to all intramural staff members regarding procedures to be followed in emergency situations (injuries).   1 2 3 4 5 6 7

Physical Education Facility Evaluation

In the introductory chapters of this manual the authors expounded the philosophy held by most educators in America for many decades that athletics should be considered a part of the total physical education curriculum in schools. In most public and private schools multiple use of facilities for all facets of the physical education program (i.e., physical education, athletics, and recreation) is employed.

Since most frequently there is multiple use of facilities, it is not always convenient to evaluate facilities from a single point of view. In the text *Planning Physical Education and Athletic Facilities in Schools* by Penman (John Wiley and Sons, 1977) a comprehensive evaluation instrument is presented that may be used to evaluate the total physical education facility from elementary schools through colleges. The instrument includes: evaluation of facilities to be used for physical education from an instructional point of view, evaluation of facilities to be used for athletic competition, and evaluation of areas to be used for school recreational pursuits. After compiling data for the total physical education facility a profile is developed similar to the profile in this manual for evaluating athletic facilities. By examining the profile it can be seen where improvement in the area of facilities is most needed.

The following pages give examples of the thirty indoor and outdoor spaces included in the evaluation instrument. For those wishing to assess the total physical education facility, you may consult the Penman text.

The user of this manual, however, may wish to evaluate athletic facilities separately. To accommodate these users, permission has been obtained from John Wiley and Sons, publisher of the Penman text, to modify the evaluation instrument to include those sections that pertain only to athletic facilities. This instrument, with directions for using it are presented in Part Three—The Athletic Program—of this manual.

	Level			Area 1	Rating		Remarks
					1–2–3		
EL	*MS*	*HS*	*CC*	*Phys. Educ. Office*	♂	♀	*Remarks*
	X	X	X	visibility to lockers			
X	X	X	X	acoustics			
X	X	X	X	aesthetics			
X	X	X	X	telephone outside line			
X	X	X	X	intercom			
X	X	X	X	no. of desk spaces			
X	X	X	X	bulletin board			
X	X	X	X	chalkboard			
	X	X	X	master H_2O temp. cont.			
X	X	X	X	lighting			
X	X	X	X	clock			
X	X	X	X	climate control			
X	X	X	X	electric outlets			
X	X	X	X	floor surface approp.			
X	X	X	X	storage			
				locker room:			
	X	X	X	adeq. no. of lockers			
	X	X	X	showers			
	X	X	X	water closets, urinals			
	X	X	X	lavatories			
	X	X	X	mirrors			
	X	X	X	bench or chairs			
	X	X	X	refrigerator			
		X	X	film review area			

Total possible points
— 69
— 69
— 66
— 39

Total Points

(continued on the next page)

Adapted from: Penman, *Planning Physical Education and Athletic Facilities in Schools.* Copyright 1977 John Wiley and Sons. Used with permission.

PHYSICAL EDUCATION FACILITY EVALUATION (*continued*)

Level				Area 2	Rating		Remarks
					1–2–3		
EL	*MS*	*HS*	*CC*	*Phys. Educ. Locker Room*	♂	♀	*Remarks*
	X	X	X	adequate lockers			
	X	X	X	adeq. lighting-protected			
	X	X	X	drainage			
	X	X	X	bulletin board			
	X	X	X	adequate exhaust fans			
	X	X	X	benches—2 rows			
	X	X	X	drinking fountain			
	X	X	X	clock—protected			
	X	X	X	floor surface approp.			
	X	X	X	aesthetics			
	X	X	X	mirrors			
	X	X	X	acoustics			
	X	X	X	hose connection			
	X	X	X	adeq. traffic pattern			
				restroom:			
	X	X	X	lavatories			
	X	X	X	water closets, urinals			
	X	X	X	mirrors			
	X	X	X	towel storage			

Total possible points
54
54
54

Total Points

(continued on the next page)

Adapted from: Penman, *Planning Physical Education and Athletic Facilities in Schools.* Copyright 1977 John Wiley and Sons. Used with permission.

Level				Area 13	Rating		Remarks
					1-2-3		
EL	MS	HS	CC	Dance Studio	♂	♀	Remarks
	?	X	X	lighting—variable			
		X	X	acoustics			
		X	X	aesthetics			
		X	X	climate control			
		X	X	mirrors—1 wall min.			
		X	X	clock			
		X	X	elect. outlets 110-220			
		X	X	dance bars			
		X	X	portable seating			
			X	stage			
		X	X	storage costume			
				and set			
			X	workshop			
			X	staging lights			
		X	X	floor surface approp.			
		X	X	PA and AV systems			
		X	X	flexibility			
			X	dressing room or rest			
				rooms nearby			

Total possible points
51
39

Total
Points

(continued on the next page)

Level				Area 14	Rating		
					1-2-3		
EL	*MS*	*HS*	*CC*	*Multi-purpose Room*	♂	♀	*Remarks*
	X	X	X	lighting			
	X	X	X	acoustics			
	X	X	X	aesthetics			
	X	X	X	climate control			
	X	X	X	elect. outlets			
	X	X	X	chalkboard flush			
	X	X	X	bulletin board flush			
	X	X	X	blackout capability			
	X	X	X	floor surface			
	X	X	X	portable table & chairs			
	X	X	X	storage large area			
	X	X	X	clock			
	X			multistation weight			
				training machine			
			Total possible points				
			36		Total Points		
			36				
			39				

Adapted from: Penman, *Planning Physical Education and Athletic Facilities in Schools.* Copyright 1977 John Wiley and Sons. Used with permission.

PART FIVE

Appendix

POSITION ANNOUNCEMENT

Physical Education Teacher

Superintendent	Dr. Tom Mays
Principal	Dr. Richard Waters
Address	Northwest Public Schools
	1313 Airport Lane
	North Bend, Oregon 97459

Phone Number ___

JOB TITLE: *Physical Education Instructor*

STARTING DATE: August 29, 1979

PLACE: Northwest Senior High School, North Bend, Oregon (North Bend is a community of 20,000 adjacent to the city of Portland. The high school has 1,800 students.)

POSITION DESCRIPTION: The teaching assignment for this position in 1979–80 will include five periods per day in various levels of physical education. One period per day will be reserved for teacher preparation. (See attached for specific duties.)

QUALIFICATIONS: Applicants should hold a Bachelors degree in physical education and hold a valid state teaching certificate. Previous experience helpful but not required.

PREFERENCE GIVEN TO: Preference will be given to those with experience at either the junior or senior high level, and those willing to assist in coaching sports after school.

SALARY RANGE: Based on the salary schedule (1979–80 $10,150–$15,741) plus $600 for assisting in each sport.

APPLICATION PROCEDURE:

1. Write or call for district application forms.
2. Complete the forms and return them prior to the closing date along with a transcript and professional references or placement file. (Three letters of reference from previous employers could be substituted for the placement file.)
3. An interview will be scheduled only for those applicants selected as finalists by the screening committee.
4. Additional information for submitting applications, employee benefits, and any other information desired by the applicant may be obtained by contacting: Dr. Philip Hirsch, Superintendent, School District 16R, 1000 SW Colorado Blvd., Pullman, WA 99163.
5. All application materials must be received by July 1, 1979.

EQUAL OPPORTUNITY STATEMENT: District 16R is an equal opportunity employer and does not discriminate on the basis of age, race, exceptionality, color, national origin, religion, political affiliation, or sex.

JOB DESCRIPTION

Physical Education Teacher

The applicant must:
1. possess a knowledge of and the ability to teach physical education *effectively* in *high school.*
2. meet and instruct assigned classes in the locations and at the times designated. Primary responsibility will be to teach physical education at the high school level.
3. develop a course of study that, as much as possible, meets the individual needs, interests, and abilities of the students.
4. create an atmosphere, climate, or rapport that is conducive to learning and appropriate to the maturity and interests of the students.
5. prepare for classes assigned and show written evidence of preparation upon request of immediate supervisor.
6. demand that students maintain established standards of classroom behavior.
7. guide the learning process toward the achievement of curriculum goals and, in harmony with the goals, establish clear objectives for all lessons, units, projects, and to communicate these objectives to students.
8. employ a variety of instructional techniques and instructional media, consistent with the physical limitations of the location provided and the needs and capabilities of the individuals or student groups involved.
9. strive to implement by instruction and action the district's philosophy of education and instructional goals and objectives.
10. assess the accomplishments of students on a regular basis and provide progress reports as required.
11. maintain accurate, complete, and correct records as required by law, district policy, and administrative regulations.
12. diagnose the learning disabilities of students on a regular basis, seeking the assistance of the district specialist as required.
13. take all necessary and reasonable precautions to protect students, equipment, materials, and facilities.
14. make provisions for being available to students and parents for education-related purposes outside the instructional day when required or requested to do so under reasonable terms.
15. plan and supervise purposeful assignments for teacher aides and/or volunteers.
16. strive to maintain and improve professional competence (i.e., readings, attending professional meetings, etc.).
17. attend staff meetings and serve on staff committees as required.
18. assist in coaching sports requested by the district.

19. be responsible for keeping an up-to-date inventory of all physical education and playground equipment.
20. perform other such tasks and assume other such responsibilities as the building principal may from time to time assign.

POSITION ANNOUNCEMENT

Head Coach
Universal School District No. 123
Anytown, U.S.A.

JOB TITLE: *Teacher/Head (Sport) Coach*

STARTING DATE: August 1, 1978

PLACE: University High School, Anytown, U.S.A. (population 14,000). Enrollment: 1,600 students (four-year high school).

POSITION DESCRIPTION: The head coach is responsible for the organization and administration of the (sport) program, grades 9–12. The head coach is directly responsible to the athletic director and follows the rules and regulations of the school district.

Responsibilities:

1. Prepare and condition the athletes for competition.
2. Game management and practice organization.
3. Maintain proper health and safety practices.
4. Supervise assistant coaches.
5. Purchase and care of equipment.

QUALIFICATIONS: A valid state teacher's certificate is required. The successful candidate for this position will have had three to five years of successful high school head coaching experience at AAA level or college experience. This person will have also participated in this sport at the intercollegiate level, will possess an excellent knowledge of the sport and be able to work effectively with high school athletes.

PREFERENCE GIVEN: Preference will be given to candidates who are also qualified to serve as assistant coach in another sport and teach in an academic area.

SALARY: $1,800 coaching stipend for head coach in addition to teaching salary. $1,200 coaching stipend for assistant (sport) position.

APPLICATION PROCEDURE: The application for this position is to be submitted to the District Personnel Director, 123 Fourth St., Anytown, U.S.A. 56789, and received no later than 5:00 p.m., Friday, May 26, 1978. Applications and additional information may be obtained from this office or by calling (998) 765-3421.

EQUAL OPPORTUNITY STATEMENT: Applications from all people are welcomed, and members of minority groups are especially encouraged to apply. The University School District does not discriminate on the basis of race, color, religion, national origin, sex, age, or exceptionality in employment or in the admission to or operation of its educational programs or activities, as required by Titles VI and VII of the Civil Rights Act of 1964, Title IX of the Education Amendments of 1972, Executive Order 11246 as amended, the Vocational Rehabilitation Act of 1973, and other state and federal laws and regulations.

JOB DESCRIPTION

Head Coach

I. REPORTS TO: Athletic director
II. SUPERVISES: Assistant coaches, trainer, and student assistants
III. BASIC FUNCTION: To provide leadership, supervision, and organization of a specific athletic activity, and to carry out the objectives of the total athletic program.
IV. PRIMARY RESPONSIBILITIES:
   A. Year-round Responsibilities
      1. Formulate objectives for the coming sport season.
      2. Keep abreast of new ideas and techniques by attending clinics and workshops, reading in his/her field and encouraging the assistant coaches to do the same.
      3. Be knowledgeable of rules and regulations concerning his/her sport.
      4. Keep abreast of rule changes in his/her sport.
      5. Implement proper procedures for out-of-season practices according to state high school association guidelines.
      6. Be active in professional organizations such as the state coaches association.
      7. Inventory, selection, care and maintenance of equipment.
      8. Assists the athletic director as needed.
   B. Seasonal Responsibilities
      1. Before Season
         a. Assist athletic director with proper registration of all athletes.
         b. Assist athletic director in the payment of necessary fees.
         c. Review the district policy on accident reporting and insurance procedures.
         d. Assist athletic director in compiling eligibility lists and other reports.
         e. Post an emergency phone and doctors list.
         f. Arrange for a systematic issuance of school equipment.
         g. Make sure all athletes have had physicals.
         h. Explain all regulations of the district presented in the Players' Handbook.
         i. Clarify to athletes the letter award policy.
         j. Select and instruct team managers on proper care of equipment, facilities, and other duties as assigned.
         k. Check arrangements for all bus trips with athletic director.
      2. During Season
         a. Assume responsibility for constant care of equipment and facilities being used.
         b. Assume supervisory control over all phases of teams in the program.
         c. Organize and schedule practice sessions on a regular basis with the idea of developing the athlete's greatest potential.
         d. Apply discipline in a firm and positive manner as outlined according to athletic policy.

e. See that facility regulations are understood and enforced.

f. Emphasize safety precautions and use accepted training and injury procedures.

g. Conduct oneself and teams in an ethical manner during practice and in contests.

h. Report outcome of contest to the media.

i. Instruct players on rules and rule changes, and new ideas and techniques.

j. Provide to the athletic director for file purposes a copy of all general correspondence and bulletins to student athletes and parents.

k. Adhere to the rules and regulations of the school district regarding school bus regulations.

l. File a discipline report with the athletic director when applicable.

m. Directly supervise or designate a supervisor of all dressing rooms and shall lock up all facilities at the close of each practice or contest.

n. Accompany and direct the varsity team in all interscholastic activities at home and assistant coaches at such activities.

o. Designate one or more of assistant coaches to be responsible for the junior varsity team and freshman team.

3. End of Season

a. Arrange for the systematic return of all school equipment and hold the athlete responsible for all equipment not returned.

b. Arrange for cleaning, storing, and conducting an inventory of all equipment.

c. Recommend student athletes who have fulfilled requirements for athletic letters, certificates or special awards.

d. Recommend additions and/or improvements for the care and maintenance of facilities.

e. Recommend to the athletic director and principal, personnel for assistant coaching positions.

f. Submit recommendations for schedule for next year.

g. Select equipment and make recommendations for purchases of such.

h. Prepare a budget in conjunction with the athletic director.

i. Maintain records of team and individual accomplishments.

j. Evaluate past season.

POSITION ANNOUNCEMENT

Assistant Coach

JOB TITLE: *Assistant Women's Basketball Coach*
STARTING DATE: August 23, 1978
PLACE: West Marlin, Montana (West Marlin is a small community approximately fifty miles north of Billings. The high school has approximately 400 students.)
POSITION DESCRIPTION: The assistant coach will assist the head coach in all phases of the program including coaching the junior varsity team. Teaching in academic areas will also be required.
QUALIFICATIONS: Experience preferred in playing and coaching the sport of basketball. Successful teaching experience is also required.
SALARY: Salary is commensurate with experience and degrees. The District base teaching salary is $10,000. Assistant coaches receive an additional $600 for each sport.
APPLICATION PROCEDURE:
Request an application and send placement papers to:
J.K. Norman, Superintendent of Schools
West Marlin School District
West Marlin, Montana
Deadline for all application material is July 31, 1978. West Marlin School District is an equal opportunity employer.

JOB DESCRIPTION

Assistant Coach, Women's Basketball

The responsibilities below are the prime concerns of the assistant coach. As the program develops it may be necessary to alter or add responsibilities to meet the needs of the total program.

The assistant coach in the women's basketball program will be responsible for:

GENERAL RESPONSIBILITIES

1. Promoting the worth of each participant in the program.
2. Displaying school and program support to incoming players, parents, and personnel.
3. Assisting in the development of the total women's sports program.

SPECIFIC RESPONSIBILITIES

1. Floor coaching of the junior varsity team.
2. Assisting head coach in floor coaching of the varsity team.
3. Delegation of duties to team managers:
    a. uniforms
    b. equipment
    c. scorebooks and reports to press
    d. statistics
4. Locker room supervision before and after games.
5. Assisting with spring and summer conditioning programs.
6. Assisting junior high coaches with development of basketball program.
7. Assisting head coach in duties he/she deems necessary.
8. Support the head coach by abiding by specific rules related to coaching duties, routine, etc. off season meeting, etc.

POSITION ANNOUNCEMENT

Physical Education Instructor
and
Coordinator of Athletics

NORTHERN UNIVERSITY
Coldspot, Minnesota 45000
Phone: 800-200-2222

RESPONSIBILITIES: Teach physical education courses. Coordinate the athletic program and coach athletic teams. Academic competency in physical education required and teaching experience preferred. Coaching ability and interest in women's athletics required. Coaching competencies required.

QUALIFICATIONS: Ph.D. desired, M.A. or equivalent required.

ACADEMIC RANK: Based on qualifications and experience.

AVAILABLE: September, 1977.

COMPENSATION: Competitive, based upon qualifications. Fringe benefits include TIAA/CREF after one year, medical and life insurance, tuition remission for spouse and children attending Northern. AAUP ratings for 1975–76 are 3 for assistant professor, 2 for associate professor, and 2 for professor.

EQUAL OPPORTUNITY: Northern University is an equal opportunity employer and all applications will be considered on their merits. A woman is sought for the position and preference will be given to women applicants.

DESCRIPTIVE INFORMATION: Northern University is a coeducational, residential, liberal arts college of about 600 students. It is a member of the Associated Colleges of the Midwest and is related to the United Presbyterian Church. The university offers the Bachelor of Arts degree in twenty departmental majors as well as topical, divisional and general majors. The College has an excellent plant, the Smith Library, and the Smith Coliseum and Center being the newest facilities. Faculty research is encouraged, but the major concern is for effective teaching and for positive relations with students. Coldspot is a community of 11,000 population, which is located about 200 miles southwest of Winnipeg. There is Amtrak service to Minneapolis, and air service from Twin Cities, Chicago, and Milwaukee. The area surrounding Northern is one of the richest agricultural areas in the country.

DEPARTMENT AND ATHLETICS: The Physical Education Department consists of five faculty members who also coach plus part-time coaches and general assistants. A physical education major is offered. Intercollegiate sports for men include football, cross country, soccer, basketball, wrestling, swimming, baseball, track, golf, and tennis. Intercollegiate sports for women include tennis, volleyball, basketball, softball. Northern is a member of the NCAA, AIAW, and the Midwest Intercollegiate Athletic Conference.

305

BIOGRAPHICAL ACADEMIC DATA: Interested applicants should have curriculum vita, including undergraduate and graduate academic records, and letters of recommendation from persons who know the quality of work accomplished and who have a basis for judging the individual's potential, sent to:

Dean John Smith
Dean of the College
Northern University
Coldspot, Minnesota 45000

POSITION ANNOUNCEMENT

Athletic Trainer for Women's Athletics with Teaching Responsibilities in the Department of Health, Physical Education, and Recreation

NORTHERN UNIVERSITY
Coldspot, Minnesota 45000

TERM OF APPOINTMENT: 9 month appointment.

SALARY: $9,000–$11,000.

QUALIFICATIONS: 1. NATA Certification.
2. Progress towards Master's Degree.
3. Two years of experience at the college level.

RESPONSIBILITIES:
1. Athletic trainer for all women's athletic teams.
2. Work cooperatively with the men's trainer and assist with the men's athletic teams when possible.
3. Instruct courses related to the field of athletic training.
4. Prepare budget for training supplies.
5. Keep medical records on all female athletes.

APPLICATION DEADLINE: May 20, 1977.

Send letter of application, including vita or resume, undergraduate and graduate transcripts and letters of recommendation supporting candidacy for this position to:

Mr. M.D. Taper
Director of Athletics
Northern University
Coldspot, MI 45000
Phone: 800-200-2222

The above material must reach NU by May 20 for your application to be considered.

GENERAL INFORMATION: Northern University is located in Coldspot, Minnesota with a student enrollment of 8,000 students. The school is a tax assisted institution and draws students from Michigan, Wisconsin, Illinois, Indiana, Ohio, Minnesota, and other states within the continental United States. Northern is well known for its teacher education programs and other related educational offerings. Northern University is a member of the NCAA-Division II and AIAW.

NEW HPER BUILDING: A new ten million dollar Health, Physical Education, and Recreational facility that opened in December 1976 has well equipped classrooms, laboratories, and activity areas that provide an excellent teaching and coaching and learning environment.

Northern University is an Equal Opportunity, Affirmative Action Employer.

JOB DESCRIPTION

Instructor of Physical Education and Women's Athletic Trainer

DEPARTMENT OF ATHLETICS
NORTHERN UNIVERSITY
Coldspot, Minnesota 45000

This staff member will be responsible for teaching skill classes in the physical education program as assigned by the head of the physical education division.

The responsibilities of the women's athletic trainer include:

1. Being available prior to, during and after all team workouts and home contests.
2. Evaluating injuries and physical conditions and making recommendations for medical attention when deemed necessary.
3. Administering treatment as prescribed by the NU medical department.
4. Preparing athletes for activity when specific care is necessary to protect the athlete.
5. Consulting with coaches regarding the status of athletes receiving care from the trainer.
6. Keeping the coach informed regarding the condition of athletes who have sustained injuries and have been treated by NU medical personnel (physician and/or trainer).

The women's athletic trainer reports to the women's athletic director on matters of policy and to the head trainer on medical matters.

POSITION ANNOUNCEMENT

Physical Education Department Chairperson

METROPOLITAN UNIVERSITY
College of Health, Physical Education, and Recreation
Metropolitan, USA 99000

DATE NOTICE: February 1, 1977	POSITION: Department Chairperson, Physical Education three-year position with reappointment procedures (nine-month appointment with Summer School option)
APPLICATION DEADLINE: April 15, 1977	
DATE OF APPOINTMENT: September, 1977	
APPLY TO: Dr. John Smith Chairman Search Committee Physical Education Department 1000 University Drive Metropolitan University Metropolitan, USA 99000	RANK: Professor or Associate Professor Commensurate with experience and professional qualifications. Position is tenured.
	SALARY: Commensurate with experience and professional qualifications.

POSITION DESCRIPTION:
1. Provide administrative and academic leadership for the department.
2. Plan, manage, and execute budget and programs in graduate, undergraduate, intramural, and service course areas.
3. Foster creativity and utilize staff in organized and uniquely diversified programs, encouraging innovative approaches toward program planning and evaluation.
4. Promote scholarly activity in the areas of personal and professional interests of faculty and encourage research and development.
5. Act as a public relations liaison between the department of physical education and the college of HPE&R, the university and the larger community.
6. Maintain relationship with local, state, and nationally affiliated organizations.
7. Perform additional duties as assigned by the University Administration or the Dean of the college of HPE&R.

DESIRABLE EDUCATIONAL AND
EXPERIENTIAL QUALIFICATIONS:
1. Earned doctorate.
2. Experience in teaching in the elementary or secondary levels.
3. Experience in teaching in higher education.
4. Administrative experience in higher education in personnel, budget, curriculum, or related areas.

5. Proficiency and experience in teacher education programs.
6. Experience in the graduate program.
7. Personal competence in or adequate knowledge of research development.
8. Demonstrated ability to work with people and leadership capabilities.

RELATED INFORMATION:

1. The Department of Physical Education combines men's and women's programs and offers Bachelor's, Master's and Doctorate (Ph.D. and Ed.D.) degrees.

Number of faculty members	40
Number of undergraduate majors	500
Number of graduate majors	175
Numbers of graduate teaching fellows	60

2. Metropolitan University has an enrollment of 16,500.
3. Population in the "greater metropolitan area" approximates 200,000.
4. Metropolitan is located close to mountains, rivers, and is surrounded by lakes. Hunting, fishing, and skiing are outstanding.

Official notification of appointment will be made by June 1, 1977. The Metropolitan University is an Affirmative Action/Equal Opportunity, Title IX Institution.